The Comic History of Ireland

EDWARD J. DELANEY AND
JOHN M. FEEHAN

Containing 9 invasions (assorted), several Rebellions (mixed), many good battles (fierce), 11 Feasts (with treachery), and several other sporting events.

ILLUSTRATED BY JEROME SULLIVAN

THE MERCIER PRESS
4 BRIDGE STREET, CORK

This edition is an abbreviation of the two volumes of *The Comic History of Ireland* published in 1951.
© The Mercier Press

Reprinted 1964, 1967, 1969, 1972, 1976
SBN 85342 058 0

Reprinted Photo-Litho in the Republic of Ireland

DEDICATION

To the history students of Ireland who
make history – when they need it!

PRESS OPINIONS

ACKNOWLEDGMENTS

Much of the material of this book has already appeared on the backs
of envelopes, cigarette packets, snaps, sweet bags, creamerybooks,
rate demand notices, E.S.B. bills, pawn tickets, and ice cream wafers,
and is now reproduced here by courtesy of the owners.

FOREWORD

We, the sole authors of this epoch-marked little book, are proud to be able to put humbly before you, from hitherto untapped sources (as well as tapped ones) the first unauthenticated history of our island isle. We also present it to you as a work (unlike all other histories) which is entirely unbiassed, unembellished, unvarnished, unwhitewashed, undistempered, and unique.

For the better understanding of this history, the reader, be he superficial, learned, or just plain ignorant, ought to be told that our qualifications to produce such a work are practically nil. Niggardly Nature has meanly denied us the streams of consciousness and the consequent abysmal obscurity which constitute the transcendent beauty of our most noted Anglo-Irish literature of to-day; a beauty which transports the hairy highbrow of London, Paris, Philadelphia or Portnamuck into the seventeenth Heaven of artistic ecstasy.

We have, however, the advantage of a good education, garnered mostly at the annual dinners of our Past Pupils' Union, at which we are much uplifted by being informed yearly of the intellectual, national, physical, psychological, moral, and social benefits which were long ago conferred upon us by precept, example and a cane; but this, unfortunately, was achieved during the best years of our lives, when we were too happy to appreciate or even notice it.

Nevertheless, it is to these happy years that we now return for our inspiration. Mindful of our own earnest if segregated efforts to capture the hearts and marks of our captious examiners in the past, we have made many successful sorties into our school answer sheets of our brighter history students of the present. History of the variety which you will find in these pregnant pages is not manufactured on the battle-fronts of a war-torn world, nor on the playing-fields of an arbitrarily chosen college. It is gouged out with sweat and blood and blots and even tears, in the heat of many a hard-fought examination, where every word which the sorely-pressed candidate can conscript from the elusive past is pressed into service.

In our sparkling pages (as the keener critics will call them) no reference is intended to any living or dead person, place or thing, except where names are mentioned. With that native caution so marked within the Dail and other immune places, we have chosen exclusively only those characters far too deceased to hit back. This was a simple choice, for it is to be observed in the history industry in general, that the most remarkable episodes are the work of impulsive citizens who passed on in the process of their production.

History is sometimes referred to with disrespect by people who ought to know better. 'History is bunk,' said Henry Ford, who could scarcely have seen this little book of ours. 'History is a fable agreed upon,' said Napoleon who made quite a nasty little slice of it himself by callously compelling his soldiers to walk on their own stomachs, probably with heavy field boots too. 'If a man could say nothing against a character but what he can prove,' said Samuel Johnson, 'history could not be written,' with which we too are in almost unanimous agreement.

'History never embraces more than a small part of reality,' said Rochefoucauld, which leaves us still qualifying, with strokes to spare. 'How oft we sigh,' said Tom Moore, 'to think when histories charm that histories lie.' We, too, in this charming history of ours, cannot guarantee ourselves above an occasional involuntary little lie or two, in the public interest; but we are fortified in this departure by the declaration of William Makeshift Thackeray, that 'great lies are as great as great truths, and prevail constantly, and day after day.'

History, however, we regret to say, has one tiresome habit, namely that of repeating itself, to which we never descend. Even when historians repeat one another, we stand superiorly aloof, content to repeat only our earnest students. To them, therefore, we dedicate this monumental work, for which we expect no public recognition, not even the distinction (and advertisement) of having our book banned. Though doubtless, when we are dead long enough to have our failings forgotten, but not long enough to have them dug up again, a grateful nation will do fitting homage to our memory. We will then make no objection if we are given a statue, which makes us out to have been an advanced case of elephantiasis, put up in some public square where it will impede the traffic. In the meantime, however, we prefer (with Cato) that some discerning soul may happily ask why such a statue is not set up, rather than that an unthinking multitude should irreverently enquire why it is.

E.J.D., J.M.F., Q.E.D.

Ireland

Ireland is an island with water round the edges, and land in the middle. It is the oldest land in the western world, and that is why it now needs manure.

Ireland is long noted for being green, also for being first in many things. Thus it grew the first flower of the earth; and the first sailor in the world was an Irishman, Jem of the Sea. At one time Ireland sank very low (see Butler) and this did not assist Trade, the water flowing in too far upon it, owing to the drains being choked, also to bad Government. This was known as the Drain Age, still upon us, the drains now being opened and piped, Ireland also being famous for pipers, the next Government also always being the best.

Then the earth heaved and threw Ireland up again, and the country went ahead greatly, for this assisted Trade. It threw up mountains round the edge and a bog in the middle, thus giving rise to Clonsast, the dumps in the Park, strikes, no coal, and many politics. Bogs are useful (see Old Bog Road).

Then the frost came, and Ireland was covered with Ice. All the people were under it, forty feet thick, and they could not light the Pastoral Fire, and so they all perished, being buried together in Communist graves.

This was the Cold Store Age, and it did not assist Trade, except frozen meat, now also not imported owing to meat of our own or home industry, and so the cost of living went up.

England

The coast of Ireland is broken, and this assists Trade, Ireland being fond of giving Trade to other nations, even when broke. Europe is off the east coast of Ireland, also England, but not so far off. Nevertheless, the prevailing wind in Ireland blowing towards England, assists the people of Ireland to live in spite of being near England, also noted for coal, iron, and honour.

It assists England too, blowing Irish people over to England, to do work for the English people which they do not like doing for themselves. This gives the English more time for football pools, crosswords, horses, dogs, dances, and lounge bars, the

Irish at home being also skilled in these historic pursuits. Thus is created a better understanding between the sister nations, whose interests in so many important respects are interdependent, thus helping to end Partition, still however, in a good state of preservation (see O'Neill).

Ancient Ireland

In the Dark Ages, the E.S.B. not having been thought of, Ireland was the one bright spot notwithstanding. It was famous for the following things:

LITERATURE

Writing and headline copybooks were invented by means of Fosterage, thus many important lies were preserved by the ancient Analysts for the school books. They are to be found in many ancient volumes which are highly coloured, such as the Book of the Dumb Cow, D.C., which does not say much, the Yellow Book of Termonfeckin, B.T., the Black Book of Baltinglass, P.O., and the Spotted Book of Duniry, B.D., all of which paved the way for the Blue Books of to-day.

There were also a number of Annuals, such as the Annuals of the Four-masters (all about sailing ships), the Annuals of Ulster, portion of which is lost, the Chronicum Scoforum, brought by the Picks and Scoffs, who had now become chronic: and the Psalter of Cashel, which could not be preserved because it became lost before it was written.

Also Irish History is noted for Glossaries, which could not be preserved because some of the gloss had gone off them, and because some of them were preserved already; and for Martyrologies, Tracks, Synchronisms, and Seana-Cusses. These were all written in the middle of the night by Genealogies, whose duty it was to take down the history of families when they had any and did not mind people knowing it.

These books led to many fierce wars, which were brought to an end by King Diarmuid saying aloud, 'To every cow its book, and to every calf its copyright.'

MUSIC

The chief musical instrument in ancient Ireland was the harp that once, which was really a Crot. Once Irish Music was nearly lost because of the Exactions of the Bars. The harps were played by blind beggars who, nevertheless were full of hope and love, the best known of them being Rafferty and Philly.

They had many airs like Earn The Tear, which were known as Moore's Melodies, because they were invented by men like Bunty and Thomas Moore before they were lost for ever. They harped on feast days, on wet days, on the weather in general, on the crops and the state of the country and the cost of living. Harping is still carried on in Ireland. The best harpers were also known as Angashores.

The last of the Bars was O'Carolans. Columcille once made history by walking blindfolded from Iona Road to settle the

Striking Terror

question of the Bars. There were also the bagpipes, being used when marching to battle to strike terror into the hearts of the enemy.

ART

Ancient Ireland was full of Art like Tara Brooches, gargoyles, gorgers, fabulaes, fibulaes, methers, blethers, torques and barques, which were worn round the neck or on the ankles. Many of the Tara brooches are still in a good state of preservation and they are eagerly sold in the shops to tourists, Other Irish antipathies were querns, cromlechs, dolmens, cumals and the ollamh fodhla: and that is why Ireland is full of art to-day, like A Flood in Donegal, A Boghole in Connemara, A Cesspool in Kilmucklin, Backyards in the Coombe, and Hens in the Rain.

11

LAW

Irish Law was invented by a Firbolg solicitor, whose name was Brehon Coad. The chief part of Irish Law was a fine colled Eric, which could be paid little by little to the man who was murdered, and if he refused to take it that way he could be killed for nothing. This was known as the Instalment System, which was due to Lughaidh Lamh Fhada, now also well known as Long-Finger Louis.

Long Finger Louis

According to Irish Law of the time nobody could cut a stick in a fort, look at a magpie, or take a red-haired woman with two left legs on a journey. When the Fesh More at Tara was held no man was allowed to injure or kill a neighbour until it was over. Sometimes a prisoner was made to swallow a redhot iron to see if he were guilty. This was known as Trial By Error.

SOCIETY

Society when there was any was divided into Flaiths, saer-ceiles, daer-ceiles, flanns, bo-aires, mol-aires, aires and graces. The flaiths could wear long hair and as many clothes as they liked. The others could wear less clothes according to their station. Graces and aires had to cut their hair short. Molaires could have no hair at all, and they should be free from personal blemish, defect or informity for they were allowed hardly any clothes at all. If a mol-aire also were found to be over-dressed he could be stripped off and galloped through the main street on a white horse. This was an old custom brought over from England (like many fine customs of to-day) and it was known as 'The Mean Test,' from Lady Boadicea on a

Less Clothes

white horse with no saddle or clothes, who did not mean it, only reducing, namely the rates.

DEATH AND BURIAL

There were two kinds of soldiers in ancient Ireland, Glasgow-glasses or heavy soldiers (16 stone and over) who followed the Picks and Scoffs from Glasgow. They fought with hatchets and

Arms in his hands

they were so powerful that they had to kill the stoutest enemy but once. The Cairns were lighthearted soldiers from Drogheda, who had very small arms. They fought with yellow or suffering tunics, skeins, and javelins tied to the fongs of their boots, which lost them many a battle. When a king died he was forced to stand up in the grave with his arms in his hands. The poor were burned to make sure that they would never come back, and their ashes were placed in Urns on the top of a hill. When seven were placed together in a pile the hill was called a cumulus, the bodies of the rich also sometimes being incriminated, in creatoriums.

COLONIES

There were many colonies in ancient Ireland, and that is what caused the Irish Race. They were:

The Ceasaireans, led by Lady Ceasair and her fifty children, some of whom had grown up in the meantime. They came to Ireland at the beginning of The Deluge. Because they were grumbling about the weather the Pagan gods were Insensed and Curst them, and so they were all drowned hand and foot in Lough Howl. The rest of them were carried off by a plague.

The Parthalonians, led by Parthalonia, who were suspected by the old Analysts to be parthily from Grease. They gathered an army but before they could fight a fierce battle they were all carried off by a plague. The rest of their story is lost in the mists of Antipathy.

The Nemedians, led by Nemesis, came from Scythia where they had invented scythes and so they had to go on their keeping. They were harassed in turn but they gathered an army and fought a fierce battle, and they were all carried off by a plague. The rest of their story is lost.

The Fomorians let by Fomoria, settled in seaside places and harassed the natives, but the natives harassed them worse, an old custom still to be found in seaside places. By then the Fomorians were too weak to fight a fierce battle, and they were all carried off by a plague.

The Firbolgs or Bagsmen, led by Firbo, drew clay in their plus-fours to the top of the Wicklow Mountains to make it the Garden of Ireland. They were all carried off by a plague, upon

Firbolgs

which their descendants at once flew post haste to England. They founded a school of thoughts in Oxford, upon which they were known as Bags (Oxon.). They were all carried off by a plague.

The Tuatha de Dannans, led by Tuatha, were magicians who

could make Irish Mist out of nothing. They marched through the bogs to Leitrim and fought a fierce battle against the enemy with spells and incarnations for two months and 94 days, until they became vague. They were all carried off by a plague and the rest of their story is lost in the Mists, thus causing the Mist that does be on the bog.

The Militians, led by Militia, landed in North Cork in a furious tempest, got up as the old Analysts say, by a de Danann play-actor named Phosferous and his beautiful daughter Veranda. Five of the eight brothers perished, and the others were cold enough too. So, singing 'Oh where's the Oil we've seen in dreams,' to keep up their spirits they set sail once more, swept the Atlantic Wave, and landed in the North by a stratagem, namely cutting off their two hands at the wrists and throwing them ashore, thus causing the Red Hand of Ulster.

CELTS

So the de Dannans, seeing that their cause was a failure, retired into the forts and started shoemaking, which assited Trade, and saved their money, which gave rise to The Crock of Gold.

Some called the Militians Celts, and others called them other things. They were the first Fior-Gaels, and they caused the Celtic Twilight. They made strong laws, under which every-

The Celtic Twilight

body had to speak compulsory Irish but themselves, thus causing the Gaelic Leak, which is still in a good state of preservation. They also invented Government of the people by the people for the people which meant that never were so many so bullied by so few. This was the beginning of the true Irish race, because they were not carried off by a plague.

PAGAN KINGS

There were many Pagan Kings at that time, including Connn the Hungry Fighter who split Ireland in two unequal halves by means of sandpits running through the country, or Esther Reidy. Low Nougat took the lower half for himself, preferring with great prudence to remain south of Esther Reidy. The country prospered greatly in his time and he assisted Trade, which is still in a good state of preservation, R.I.P., also The Cost of Living went up.

MCCORMACK MCCART

His Grandfather being Connn the Hundredth Piker, was a powerful King, having written a Book. Having, however, unfree from Physic, Defect, Blemish, or Informality according to Ancient Law, namely a Sty in his eye, he was obliged to rise out of being King, muttering fierce royal war cries aloud near the Boyne in Gaeilge na Midh. It is related of him by the Old Chronics of the time that he sent messengers to the Druids to say aloud 'I do not care for Crumb Crook nor your sub-Idles Twelve which are but Carven Treene.' Whereupon the Druids becoming Insensed curst him, and so he was drowned by a flood in his coffin while poaching a salmon at Rosnaree, instead of at Broonabona, as the Druids would have wished him to lie if they could, and buried there. The country went ahead greatly in his time and he assisted Trade, which is still in a good state of preservation, R.I.P.

Fin Mc Hool, being a nice man, was famous chiefly for his Tummy of Knowledge from eating burned fish without a fork, by which he could tell everything that was to happen whether it was to happen or not. He was also famous chiefly for being head of the Fianna Fail or Stone of Dissentry which never belonged to anybody who had it and no more does now, history having once more repeated itself as Fin's Tummy also said it would, being still in a good state of preservation, R.I.P., also the Stone now handed back having not been outside Dan

Drowned in his coffin

Murphy's door, this being known as Scotch Aspirations or Bide a Wee. Fin was also chiefly famous for chasing Diarmud O'Deeny who was chasing Granuaile, a famous jumper who was making leaps all over Ireland with Diarmuid, also Lovers' Knots including Loop Head where Diarmuid died from not getting a drink of water, Fin's hand being leaking for spite, R.I.P.

POWERFUL

Fin was also famous for being a powerful man, riding into battle on a Fenian Cycle, carrying his arms in one hand and uttering his fierce war cry with the other of 'Purity on my lips, Truth in my hands and a thorn in my foot.' Fin also wore twenty-four suffering shirts of yellow, and a crombie coat plundered without mercy from a Scottish joint, which with great prudence he fought fiercely three times running and one time galloping. Finn also jumped his own height from a Pit of spears until the Scottish joint invented the Joint's Causeway of Basic Slag for stepping stones home as he fled in terror, still in a good state of preservation. Upon which Finn, being Insensed, curst him, also cast Lough Knee after him with one mighty cast, thus giving rise to the Oil of man, the return of which

The Fenian Cycle

must be an indispensable condition of any full and final settlement of the outstanding differences between the two countries. This is a consummation to be devoutly wished for by all right-thinking people whose earnest hope it is to see cordial relations established between the sister nations, who can contribute so much each to the well-being of the other. This is known as Friendly Neighbours, still in a good state of preservation, R.I.P.

THE CHASE

Fin had two famous hounds, Bran and Pollard (30.25 and 30.25), and he used to go through the country chasing Wild Bores, also an Irish dear whose name was Ann Nelk, whom he finally caught and whose bones he placed in the Museum of Dail Eireann, where also can now be observed many other Irish antipathies, being still in a good state of preservation to remind us of the past, R.I.P.

EMIGRATION

Fin had a boy, Husheen (famous for lullabys), who set off at an early age to that fatuous land to the golden west on the edge of the azure sea, where summer is always coming, fruit is cheap, also dew on the grass, and blossoms and bees' nests, nobody ever lives to grow old, and the cost of living going down. He broke the old Irish law of Breh and Coad by going on this journey with a red-haired woman but well-dressed, Miss Neeve K. Nore, who was not an Irish National. So the Droods becoming Insensed Curst him, whereupon having said farewell to his mother-in-law, Ma Nell, he fell from his noble milkmaid steed while working in a quarry in County Wicklow, thus turning into a feeble old man on the ground, repenting all his folly and dying a happy death, R.I.P.

Husheen was also a poet and his chief work was a sad emetic poem called Laogh Husheen or The Calf of Husheen, thus giving rise to the well-known saying 'To every book its cow and to every calf its copy.'

NILE

Nile of the Nine Corsages was a powerful king, also the first man in Ireland to invent External Relations (still in a good state of perspiration), by which he attacked the Picks and Scoffs. These having returned from Scotland to Ireland and back again and viva voce, were now also known as the Spiffs and Pocks, thus bringing St. Patrick to Ireland, having almost decimated his father and mother in a fierce battle to mind pigs on Slieve Misht. Instead, St. Patrick said aloud 'Your ship is ready' in his sleep, thereby converting the Irish People at one bold stratagem by means of the pastoral Fire of Slane turf which now can never be put out in Ireland, also the pretty

External Relations

three-leaved shamrock from Glenore. St. Patrick was the first External Relation in Ireland.

BRIGHT AGES

King Dun Laoghaire, a powerful King and fior-Gael, having his name translated from Kingstown in his shirt which makes all the difference, told St. Patrick to go through the country, which he did, thus causing all the Idles to fall down with a loud cry. This improved the Health of the People, thus giving rise to Piety, Public Assemblances, Discoursions and Diabetes, Mother & Child, etc., thereby giving to Ireland the glorious name of Insulin Santorium et Doctorium, R.I.P. This was known as The Bright Ages, R.I.P., R.I.P., all snakes being banished, some creeping back however, being now in a good state of circulation in Ireland.

Appendix 1

AN ROINN OIDHEACHAIS
(Department of Education)

BRAINNSE AN MHEADHON OIDHEACHAIS
(Secondrate Education Branch)

HISTORY PAPER

Tuesday, 18th June 531, Afternoon, 12.a p.m. to 11.o a.m.
Examiner: Ollamh Cairgthneighth O Cthoighthoighth
(Professor Cairgthneighth O Cthoighthoighth)
(Answer some question for Heaven's sake)
(All the answers are of equal value)

19

1. Defame, with suitable examples, as you would to a brother Irishman, all our political leaders from 500 B.C. to the present day.

(30 marks)

2. Defend, with suitable gestures, as you would to an Englishman, all our political leaders from 500 B.C. to A.D. 5000.

(300 marks)

3. Synchronise the (1) Synchronisms of Flann, (2) the Annuals of Tighearnach, (3) the Festilologies of Feilire, (4) the Psalter of Bacon (not more than four to be attempted).

(20 marks)

4. Rewrite in Ogham the Liber Brecc (do not write on more than two sides of the paper).

(long and short marks)

5. Assemble (1) the Red Branch cycle, (2) the Fenian cycle. Which had rheumatic tyres?

(tyre marks)

6. Give with brief sketches (not more than two yards long), at least two alternatives to (1) the Brugh-fer, (2) the Muc-aire, (3) the Timpan.

(no marks)

7. Give, without malice, at least two antidotes to (1) the Lugg Age, (2) the Ethicus of Istria, (3) Queen Maeve, (4) Ma Mell.

(black marks)

8. Sing not more than four verses of 'The Crot That Once.'

(permanent marks)

9. Which half of Conn the Hungry Piker took Magh Nuadhat, and to where?

(1 electric boot lacer, 700 v.)

10. Arrange in chronological order (1) Conn the Hungry Piker, (2) his son Art, (3) his grandson Cormick Mac Airt.

(1 electric shock, 7000v.)

11. Pronounce, without misgiving or your false teeth, the following (1) Goidelic, (2) Ferleginn, (3) Log-enech, (4) Achy Feidlech, (5) Olnegmacht, (6) Tlachtgha (only one at a time to be attempted). Comment without lisping on the Ithians.

(1 blood pressure cooker)

12. Deride, without heat, the theory that the sons of Tureen invented soup.

(1 set of spoons)

13. Complete the following ancient Irish proverbs (no more than five to be attempted):

    1. Bionn ....
    2. Ni bhionn ....
    3. Is ....
    4. Ni ....

                    (1 set of spoon feeders)

14. Who was the originator of the Feis? Why is his name forgotten? Invent at least one excuse for the survival of the Feis.

                    (1 week in Gaeltacht)

15. Where was the Battle of Ocha fought (not more than three guesses permitted)?

                    (1 week in Mountjoy)

16. Explode (without spluttering) the theory that the Irish were never united.

                    (1 week in hospital)

17. Disclaim (without stuttering) the theory that St. Patrick was born in Scotland, Wales, and other places.

                    (1 easy chair)

18. 'We learn from history that we learn nothing from history.' Disprove this statement, if you have not already proved it.

                    (1 kitchen chair)

19. Trace the extent, influence, and decline of plusfours from the Fir Bolg or Bagg Age to the middle of the 20th Century.

                    (1 pair of slacks)

20. Explain (without perspiration) why the Book of Kells is in Trinity College. Discuss, whithout reference to costs of production, the price of the recent edition.

                    (1 copy of Old Moore's Almanac)

21. Describe (without wriggling) the encircling movements of Niall of the Nine Corsages at the Battle of Spirella.

                    (1 pair of nylons)

22. Enumerate the different races which came to Ireland after the Ice Age. How many of these were won by horses which were bought for a song?

                    (1 canteen of cutlery)

23. Trace diplomatically (for your own sake) the uprise, influence and domination of the Civil Service from Tuathal the Legitimate to the end of time.

                    (1 canteen)

24. Illuminate, without batting an eyelid, King Daithi's light-

ning campaign in the Alps. Give no more than ten of the chief causes which contributed to its abrupt ending.

(1 lightning conductor)

25. Comment, without restraint, on Henry Ford's observation, that 'history is bunk.' (Not more than three words to be used, of which one may be history.)

THE DANES

The Danes were divided into many parts in Ireland, including the Danes, so-called because they came from Norway, the Norsemen, so-called because they came from Denmark, the Loughlins so-called because they came from everywhere, also swarms of Hums, Gots, Sandals (from Sandinavia), Jutlings (from Jutland), Hambugs and other invaders which spread out over Europe from the Baltic Ocean like a pot of boiling water. They were also divided into Danes, Great Danes, Danes, Vikings, Olafs, Amlaffs, Anrads, Brooders and Sagars. They were a scourge, becoming too Irish for the Irish themselves.

Perished

They also went to England to try to become too English for the English themselves, in which they succeeded by a bold stratagem, putting a Danish King Canoodle up on the English Throne, washing his feet on the coasts of Kent, Surrey, Sussex, Middlesex and Kent, as was the custom in these lawless times, and crying aloud with great success as the tide reached up to his knees, 'Thus far shalt thou wash and no farther,' whereupon his flattering courtiers plunged in and perished.

BOOTY AND STOCKY

The Danes having bad tempers, strong butter, ships with flat bottoms, and long hair tucked into their waistcoat pockets, carried out Privacy on the high seas, thus cruelly plundering and slaughtering shrines and desecrating all the people, thus taking rich Booty and Stocky home in bags which is now well known as the Sack of Baltimore. This did not assist Trade

Strong

and the Cost of Living went up, and the country went ahead greatly, the next Government also always being the best.

EARLY RISERS

They came to seaside places early in the morning before the people were up, taking the milk out of the children's tea, killing all the people and ravaging. They came up the rivers and lakes in their boats with their flat bottoms, ravaging. They went into all the National Schools, tearing the covers off the precious copy books, plundering the precious stores of silver and gold, once found in Wicklow, also in the Silvermines in Tipperary—now alas! extinct, and ravaging. But try as they would they could not ravage the Round Towers, the Wolf Dogs and the Sunburst of Erin, which, thanks to the indomitable spirit of the Irish people throwing boiled water down on them from the holes in the Round Towers, remain to this date mute but silent witnesses of these ravaging times.

Boiling

The religion of the Danes was the Vallakyries in a place called Vallahalla or drinking hot blood out of the dead skulls of their enemies. They also assisted Trade, sending strong butter to people who gave away their own butter. This was known as co-operation, still in a good state of preservation, C.O.D., and the Cost of Living went up.

BRIAN BURROO

So called because he was fond of collecting Tributaries, a Fior-Gael who was really one of the Kennedys of Killaloe, being a nice man. He was also a powerful King from the County Clare which, however, is near other counties. Brian did not like the Danes, and going on the run he got on well, becoming High King of Ireland by a bold stratagem, namely sending messengers to Malachy Wore to say aloud, 'What's yours is mine and whats mine is my own and to every cow its calf.' Upon which Malachy, being a Fior-Gael and having but a small army, sent messengers back to Brian Burroo to say aloud, 'In the interests of world peace and the future welfare of the Irish nation as a whole let us sink our differences and strive together for the common weal, so take the Throne.

Rich and Rare

Which Brian unselfishly did, Malachy not wanting weals, thus uniting the country into one democratic Hole, where everybody had freedom to do what the King liked or he would have to. Brian was now busy building workhouses, jails, bridges, and Vocational Schools, for few pupils steamrolling the roads, passing Good Acts and assisting Trade, so that a girl could wonder from one end of Ireland to another in her yellow suffering dress and a gold wand on her finger singing, 'Rich and Rare were the gems she wore, without being infested or whistled after by robbers or asked where she was going or if she had anything to do at home.

BATTLE OF CLONTURF—IRISH SIDE

Brian put down the power of the Danes by the Battle of Clonturf, now known as Clontawf by the natives of that place, also in other fierce battles such as by marrying a Danish woman, Gormley, who was mother of Citric Acid of the silky Whiskers, king of Dalkey Island, who was also married to Brian's daughter, thus bringing External Relations to Ireland.

Waving their hatchets

Brian was helped by the Dalcassians (or Dail Gas), now a hurling team in Clare, who travelled in the Guard's van until the moss of the valley grew red with their blood, also on far foreign fields from Kanturk to Belgrade, now also known as Clare's Dragoons.

THE DANISH SIDE

The Danes having wrote to other Danes from the Orchids, the Chutneys, the Hebrides, the Vikings, the Synods, also swarms of Hugs, Gots, Sandals, Jutlings, Shetlings, Amlafs, Olàfs. Danegelds and Hambugs, and others sailed into Clontawf Harbour in their swift galleries with raving banners, waving their hatchets at the respectable people of Clontawf, who being more Irish than the Irish themselves did not even speak to these rude interlopers who notwithstanding and nevertheless interloped without mercy.

BRIAN SPEAKS

Brian being too feeble from passing good Acts, building workhouses, jails, bridges, Vocational Schools for few pupils, steamrolling the roads, assisting Trade, putting down robbers so that girls could wander around, did not fight himself, but made a speech which was worse for the enemy, making his men mad to rush off and kill somebody while the day was fine, they being told by Brian that the age-old struggle must go on until the invader was driven from the soil or clay of their native land, and a Dane in Ireland would be as rare as a Red Indian on the plains of Broadway. They were also told to think of the history of their country, now also learned·in school, of Emmet, Wolf Tone, O'Connell Aboo, the Crocky Boy, the Bold Roisin Do, the Manchester Martyrs, Sarsfield at Vinegar Hill, Fenian Men and Paudh O'Donoghue, also the Stone outside Dan Murphy's door, not the Lia Fault, with which to smight the Danes by land, sea and air, and every other place. Whereupon he started the battle and went back to his tent to listen in.

THE BATTLE

The Irish, singing 'Step Together,' rushed upon the Danes, also decimating them to a man, upon which the Danes, now in a good state of perspiration, seeing resistance useless, began to start back to their galleries in the harbour by which the Irish won. King Brian's son Murrough, however, met with a sad accident, also fatal, being angrily stabbed by a vexed Dane whom he had just fiercely decimated. Turlough, son of Murrough, also lost his life in a sad accident, also fatal, having

Entangled

entangled his feet in the hair of a Dane in the Dodderer. swimming home, thus getting cramps, the verdict being anonymous of drowning by exfixiation, R.I.P.

BRIAN'S DEATH

Brian also lost his life on that same evening in a sad accident, also fatal, by means of Brooder, a great Dane passing home from the battle in bad humour, and seeing the King playing in his tent. One word having borrowed another, the row arose, Brooder taking an unfair advantage with his hatchet on the King's head, the King not being looking, being busy cutting off Brooder's legs. This gave rise to the King being dead to the

Bad Humour

world and Brooder footless, not having a leg to stand on, or walk. The Battle of Clontawf is a popular battle, being easy to remember, therefore good for marks.

LOSS

Brian's death was a loss to Ireland on account of his being good at passing good acts, building jails, workhouses, bridges, vocational schools for few pupils, steamrolling the roads, assisting Trade, inflicting robbers with wandering girls, etc. Also coming of fine old agricultural stock his death cast a gloom. The cortege which followed his remains to his last resting place was large and representative, and testified in no uncertain manner to the esteem in which the diseased was held by all creeds and classes, being buried in Ulster with green, white and gold or orange, or yellow, R.U.C.

Appendix II

(Extract from *Dublin Evening Intelligence*, Friday, April 23rd, 1014.)

Brian and his men were early astir this morning. When our special correspondent visited the camp at 6.0 a.m. (S.T.) the smell of sizzling bacon and eggs hung heavy in the air, and the men, having made a hearty breakfast, were assembling to hear the King's final address. The following is the text of the King's speech, supplied exclusively to the representative of the *Evening Intelligencer:*

'Fellow-countrymen—I mean, A Chairde go Leir—I have but few words to say to you on this momentous, I might say, historic morning, for I do not intend to stand between you and the Danes. It would not, I am sure, be a healthy place to stand

27

(laughter). I know that, having been given the tools, you are now eager to finish the job. The enemy with his tattered lackey Mailmora, at his heels, is grim in hate, eager for slaughter, fierce and ruthless on the field of battle. He is equipped with the most modern and deadly engines of war, including the coat of mail, which perverted science has been able to devise. The whole land of England groans under his iron heel; he has taken the fairest province in all France for his own; he has driven deep inroads into the Baltic Countries, Italy and the Ukraine.

Will you tremble before this savage scourer of the seas, this relentless desecrator of your hallowed shrines, this merciless destroyer of the homes and altars of your sires? (*Cries of No, No.*) Will you be intimidated by his subtle propaganda, his fifth-column activities, his vainglorious boast of secret weapons? (*No, No.*) Will you quail before him as did the weak spineless Saxon,* and yield your historic land to Danish domination? (*No, No.*) Will you permit the fierce pagan to rule your beloved country, as he now rules England, even to order the very waves of your seas about? (*No, No.*) Will you stand by and watch paganistic Communism blot out everything you hold dear? (*No, No.*) Will you go on eating uneatable Danish butter while your own cows and dairymaids languish in the fertile meadows of your ancient land. (*Fierce cries of 'Never.'*)

My Countrymen, we have no quarrel with the Danes as such. We will even welcome them to our land—as tourists only. But we are firm believers in the right of small nations to decide their own destiny, and we will insist upon deciding ours (*hear, hear*). History, my friends, is in the making (*groans*). We have made plenty of it already—we will make more do-day. The year of 1014 is one which will be remembered with particular pride—and, may I venture to prophesy, without particular difficulty—by future generations of Irish students (*deep groans*).

I, my fellow-countrymen, am but a mere Clareman, like so many of yourselves (*no, no*). But from my childhood days I have struggled without ceasing, against the implacable Saxon— I mean the implacable Dane. Sooner than bend the knee I have taken to the woods and glens and wild fastnesses of my native county. I have endured toil and hardship from Shcarriff† in the east to Kilbaha in the west, I have slept on hard knotty roots, even on beds in the lodges and boarding-houses of Kilkee,

---

* Probably ancient name for English.
† Probably ancient name of Scarriff.

28

and I have risen, stiff perhaps in the joints, but stiffer in my determination to rid my country of these blood-soaked barbarians (*loud applause*).

For a thousand years, my fellow-countrymen, our indomitable ancestors have kept our illustrious island free of foreign invaders. It is not hereditary to us to submit (*hear, hear*). It is not hereditary to us to desist, until a Dane in Ireland will be as rare as a rheumatic farmer on the seats of Lisdoonvarna (*hear, hear*).

We have now, my friends, reached the end of the beginning (*hear, hear*). Upon this battle depends the future of Christian civilisation, the future of our beloved country for generations yet untold. Do we not owe a debt to posterity, to rid it of this inhuman scourge which would destroy it ere it is born (*yes, yes*)? Will your deeds to-day be an inspiration to the immortal men of future ages, Emmet, Tone, Sarsfield, O'Donnell, O'Neill, and others too numerous to mention? Will you prove worthy to rank with these peerless patriots of the future, whose incomparable deeds will add lustre to the already scintillating pages of Ireland's imperishable story? (*yes, yes*).

My countrymen, the die is cast—the issue is joined. Kathleen Ni Houlihan is at the cross-roads—alone—and patiently waiting—but not in vain. She has faithful followers, who will joyfully lead her from that wind-swept spot into the broad sunlit uplands from where she will move forward proudly to her inevitable destiny (*hear, hear*). Out yonder, my countrymen, waits the Saxon—I mean, the Danish foe. The whole fury and might of his powerful army must soon be turned upon us. Let us, therefore, brace ourselves to the task in hand, and so bear ourselves that if our proud race should last that thousand years men will still say, 'This was their finest hour!' (*prolonged applause*).

My countrymen, I have almost done. My lamp of life is nearly extinguished (*no, no*). The grave opens to receive me, and soon I must sink into its bosom (*no, no*). This is probably the last occasion on which I shall have the proud privilege of addressing you. It is inevitable, my people, in a struggle of this strenuous nature, that some should be called upon to make the supreme sacrifice, a fact of which I, who have guided your destinies for so long, have not been entirely unmindful. Consequently, I am happy to be able to announce that a far-reaching and comprehensive scheme of Social Welfare is even at this moment under active consideration; and those who lay down their lives for their beloved country can do so with perfect confidence in the future, secure in the certain knowledge that a grateful nation will make liberal provision for the needs of their loving dependents (*hear, hear*).

I would like, before we depart, to express our deep appreciation of the thoughtfulness of those public bodies who gave us such a spontaneous welcome on our arrival here in our capital city. A special word of thanks is due to our brethren of the Claremen's Association in Baile Atha Cliath,* whose help, advice, and subscriptions have been a beacon light to us in our arduous preparation for the sombre task which lies before us (*hear, hear*).

I would like too, to say a special word of thanks to our redoubtable ally and my old friend, Malachy Wore, of the Eastern Command, for his enthusiastic co-operation here to-day (*hear, hear*). We kings are human (*no, no*). We have our little disagreements, but when it comes to the supreme test Malachy's valued counsel and trusty sword have ever been mine to call upon; and I sincerely trust that the historian of the future will grant him his due meed of credit (*hear, hear*).

My countrymen, I have done (*hear, hear*). My prayers and hopes are with you, and there is a running buffet beside my tent, where refreshments will be free throughout the day. Let, therefore, your victorious laughter ring out the knell of the vanquished enemy. Your efforts to-day, and yours alone, will make Ireland a land fit for heroes to live in, a land in which, in the sunset of your declining years, sweetened by a good Government pension, you can shoulder your crutch and tell how fields were won (*wild and prolonged cheering*).

KINGS WITH PROPOSITIONS

Ireland now suffered from too much Kings with long geological tables of ancestors or four bears, each proposing to rule at the same time or each after the other or before him as the case may be or viva voce or each to each, thus giving rise to their being called Kings With Propositions. This was a disturbed period in our history, for the country did not go ahead greatly and this did not assist Trade, besides which from having too many kings it is difficult to remember, and so we pass over it lightly but sadly, R.I.P., except Roderick O'Connor who was a good swimmer, also the Cost of Living went up now also, due to causes outside nobody's control, a new Government also being always reducing it, R.I.P.

* Probably ancient name of Dublin.

THE NORMANS

The Normans lived in France where they were unsettled, having descended a long way from the Danes, coming down through the Low Countries into France. They are sometimes confused with the Mormons, now extinct from eating salt meat and too many wives in Salt Lake City. The Normans soon became civilised, thus becoming fierce bloody fighters with new and deadly weapons including archery, being more arch than the Irish themselves. They also had iron clothes, called Coats of Male to distinguish them from the Gentil Sects or Parfit Night, this being the age of Shivalry (pro. Chivalry). They also had some defects including speech, being unable to say 'the,' thus giving rise to de Clare, de Courcy, de Burgs, de Gross, de Cogan, de Lacy, de Murrage and de Oders, also de Normans, many also settling in remote places in Cork, now also to be found dere to dis day. The Normans gave rise to Castles to look at, thus being the cause of Tourists.

KIND HEARTS

De Normans seeing de plight of de English who were un-civilised (still in a good state of preservation) fired arrows in de air as at Agincourt of de Black Prince until de Sun was blotted out; and under cover of de darkness advanced hand over hand hastily into Hastings under William de Horse Chestnut. Thus they civilised England at one fell blow namely 1066, thereby hoisting William de Conkers on the throne to rule wisely and well by means of Curfew, the Salic Law, the Doodler's Book and other bold Stratagems. William was now busy telling the people to speak compulsory French, thus becoming more French than De Normans themselves, also building abbeys on robbed lands and making many saints. This glorious period of English history, in which the English nation happily disappeared, being decimated, annalated, and their remains turned into villeins (pro. villains) is now also known as 'kind hearts are more than Coroners and simple fate in Norman blood' by Shakespeare, R.I.P., being now also Dis-eased, or Bacon.

DIARMUID OF THE GALL

So called because he had more gall than any man in Ireland, was not a nice man. He was the first non-fior-Gael in Ireland, going to Landsdowne Road with a daughter, Princess Eva, on account of which he promised the two halves of his kingdom and his daughter to the first man who would make her smile in marriage.

Diarmuid being large and hoarse from shouting at Devorgilla, who was Devastating, following him through the whole of Ireland with her fortune, namely four hundred heads of cows, thus gave rise again to the old saying, 'To every cow's head its calf, etc.' She also being only forty while Diarmuid was sixty thus gave rise to romantic Ireland not being dead and gone by O'Leary, R.I.P., also Yeats, R.I.P. Thus sorely pressed by Devorgilla being devastating, Diarmuid hoarsely applied for Succer to King Henry, the Norman King of England and English King of France. Upon which Henry, a fior-Norman, being seized with pity, told Diarmuid to gather Normans in England to civilise the Irish. This Diarmuid did by Fits and a

Unsmiling

letter including Fitzstephen and Fitzgerald also Richard de Clare, Earl of Pembroke and Allbroke, also known as Strongbroke, who landed at Bansha Bay in German Submarines, fell upon his knees and upon Waterford, butchering all the people who also fell because they would not agree to be civilised. Thus Eva seeing Strongbroke in his iron clothes burst out laughing, whereupon Strongbroke at once married her in Reginald's Tower, thus becoming famous for being the fateful Norman, who never smiled again. It was a jolly wedding, with bleeding citizens filling the bloody channels, having been butchered by Raymond le Gros and Milo de Venus Cogan, to make them reasonable. This was known as The Trouble and it did not assist Trade, and the Cost of Living went up, the Government having promised to reduce it.

THE SYSTEMS

But the Normans could not civilise the Irish because of the Systems. These were:

The Clam System of the Irish, so called because the Irish wanted to stick to everything they owned, being unreasonable, biting the hands that bled them.

The Clam System

The Frugal System of the Normans which had to be, because nobody owned anything but the King, which is why the Normans having too many wives, were all broke, such as Pembroke, Bolingbroke, Carisbroke, Ladbroke, Basilbroke, Basingbroke, Broke-on-Trent, Broke-Poges etc., and so they were many Barrens being worse than Frugal. Then the Irish becoming chivalry got cots of Male too, and rushed at the Norman castles, now almost in a good state of preservation, devastating also in Dublin while swimming in the Liffey, whereupon the Normans turned white with terror, thus giving rise to their being known as The Pale. The two palest Normans were Coyne and Livery.

CRUSHER

Henry the Twice or the Second, surnamed Lackshanks, also a nice man, was a powerful King who could eat anything, this being known as the Constitution of Clarendon 1164. He was a great ruler, being able to rule England and France and everybody except his turbulent wife and children, also to crush the power of the turbulent Barrens by cutting the tails off their hounds, this being known as Scutage, also by Curia Regis and Grand Assize.

So being tired of crushing turbulent Barrens and not being able to crush his turbulent wife and children, he came to Dublin for the Horse Show, bringing the biggest Bull ever seen in Ireland. He also built a wicker-work house in Dublin thus giving rise to Housing Schemes. Also being a pleasant man, he gave parties to Irish chiefs, to tell them he wanted nothing but their lands for his Barrens. So the chiefs being fond of parties, submitted, also other chiefs homaged, fealtied and loyaltied. Upon which Henry being pleased also being a holy man had a Saint made of Thomas A. Beckett, Archbishop of Canterbury, having him piously murdered in the Cathedral. This done, he now caused a Synopsis of the Church to be held at Cashel and Waterford to plant virtue, promote the Christian religion, and if they did not agree he would let out the Bull to make them also Saints. The Cost of Living also went up due to other Causes, not the Government.

LAND DIVISION

Henry being of fine old agricultural stock, also founded the Land Commission, still in a good state of preservation, giving farms to all his friends including de Lacy, de Courcy, de Clare, de Murrage and de Oders. Whereupon he returned home, sending over his son John, surnamed Shacklanks because of his wife Magna Carta, putting heirs in the Beers of the Irish chiefs, also starting County Councils, who becoming Insensed Curst him, waving their sores in anger. Whereupon he returned home, his father dying of a turbulent wife and family and Barrens, also a surfeit of Peaches and fresh Porter, or Broken Heart, now also called Angina Pectoribus, R.I.P.

UNREASONABLE

The Irish being unreasonable because of the Clam System, would not give lands to Henry's Barrens who wanted them because of the Frugal System. They thus had nothing but what they could piously rob upon which to build Abbeys. De Courcy now being about to take Ulster (which Henry gave him) by peaceful penetration, namely force of arms, met with a fatal accident, R.I.P., by which he lost his life. De Lacy also dying suddenly, the Normans now built castles with the blood of their enemies (with no floors) in which they lived upstairs because of the ignorant Irish peeping in at them from the hills and bogs.

This was the weaning of the power of the Barrens, also Turmile.

STATUTE OF KILKENNY

The Statute of Kilkenny was in the time of Edward the Three, surnamed Shankslong, not being really a Statute but an Act of Parliament, the ignorant Irish always calling things by wrong names. About this time the English Parliament was worried because the English in Ireland were turning Irish, and the Irish in Ireland were not turning English, thus not making Ireland English for the English, but keeping it Irish for the Irish. So the English Parliament, not in Privy or Council but openly, passed an Act to be posted up on every statue in Kilkenny, now also noted for Ale, hurlers, cats and boots, and marble stones as black as ink. This Act was in thirty five parts, to keep the people from going together. This was to stop Marriage, Gossiping, Gravelkind, Tanistry, Foosterage and other Irish customs. Thus to keep the people apart they were now divided into Gulls, Shanagulls, and New Gulls. So, according to the Act no new Gull could go near a Shanagull, nor marry his wife in the open air unless she were a Gull, upon which her Black Fortune would be stopped out of her Rent.

No New Gull could wear clothes like the naked Irish. No Irish teacher could get a haircut through the medium of Irish, or wear yellow boots like the Gulls, or a fringe under his cap. No new Gull could ride a horse under the saddle or be in Croke Park or the Gaelic League, or have Irish hens, or booley cattle in an Irish boghole. No Shanagull could speak Irish when speaking English, or vidi vici. Irish bars were to be boycotted, likewise stories, pipers, Whitewashers, mowers, and cowdoctors, who were spying on the people from shore to shore, also cutting

Still a boy

hurleys, now also forbidden. But all came to nought, this being the time of Assimilation and Absorbents, the Gulls and new Gulls being Assimilated and the Shanagulls absorbed, but not in their work. This did not Assist Trade, and the country did not go ahead greatly. Also the Cost of Living went up, the Government having it under active consideration.

RICHARD THE TWO

Surnamed Sheepshanks, being a nice man, climbed up on the throne at the age of eleven while still a boy not yet in his teens. He was son of the Black Prince at Agincourt and other places, albeit washed white by his mother, upon which the people hailed him, crying aloud 'All Hail,' this being the time of hard weather. He was also related to Richard de Once or Cure de Lion, who was always going off on Cruisers to the Holy Land, also on the S.S. Berengaria, called after his wife, to fight with Saracens by chopping up iron bars with his two hands, thus striking terror into the Saracen leader Salad, making him chop the cushions with a curved samovar. Richard now being in prison was rescued by his ministrel Blondin climbing a tight rope to sing outside his cell. Richard replied in his very rich

Told to go

baritone, for Kings were well off in those days. Richard's jailers hearing him sing wept sadly, opened the gates and told him to go. Singing is useful.

Richard the Two, his motto being Itch Dien from the Black Prince, was also a King with opposition, namely Wot Toiler, Perkins Warneck, Tottenham Hotspur, and chiefly Art Mac Murrough Kavanagh, surnamed Kavanagh, being ascended from Diarmuid of the Gall, once hoarse from shouting in battle with Devorgillamore. 'Let the boy win his spurs,' he said, 'or upon it.'

CARELESS

Art becoming King of Leinster while yet a big boy in his teens was albeit a careless man, tying his horse without a saddle to the Statue of Kilkenny, also getting carelessly married to a New Gull Eliza, not keeping apart as the statue said. The English did not like Art to be married, to have issues to the Kings of Leinster, also to have his horse without a saddle scratching against the Statue of Kilkenny, and all the Nacts thereby enacted. Art broke the Acts also by being married

Scratching

without a haircut, now also up in price, also by being a member of the G.A.A. The English now took his wife's fortune, also her Black Rent, whereupon Art became black in the face, swore a loud swear to Harass, also to make the Pale paler, which he also did to them in great numbers. Black Rent was not the same however as Black Prince at Agincourt and other places.

VEXED

Richard the Two, now hearing that Art was Harassing on account of his wife's fortune escheated, her Black Rent also estreated, came to Ireland with thirty-four thousand friends, being vexed, to tell Art to stop having a wife and tissue for Kings of Leinster, also to stop going to Croke Park and having a haircut through the medium, also to stop Harassing. Learning that Art was in Wicklow, also now noted for mountains and beautiful scenery, including the Sugar Loaf and the Skelp, Richard and his friends, being fond of beautiful scenery but not of Art, walked in among the mountains, thus getting hungry, mountain air being good for the appetite, and Art having eaten all the food in the mountains. Art also swept down to the hearth of New Ross to light the town for a pastoral fire, thus carrying off rich booty and stocky. Richard was now more hungry in the mountains, also his friends, from Art digging bogholes in their way, eating the food, and swooping down.

FORGIVEN

Richard now was pleased to make peace, Art telling the proud English King, who was also vain, that he would give him all his property for nothing. This pleased the vain King, the English also being noted for being easily pleased by getting countries for nothing. So, seeing Art reasonable, the proud English King readily but magnanimously forgave Art wanting to keep his property, the English also being against killing people against fearful odds, namely The Charge of the Life

Fatal Accident

Brigade to get property. So the proud English King forthwith gave a great party (without treachery) in Dublin and soon went home with his friends who did not stay in Wicklow, except some dead ones, having met fatal accidents in Art's bogholes in the night. Bogholes are useful.

VEXED AGAIN

The native English in Ireland (not Gulls) now saw Art with no Kingdom, he having reasonably given it to Richard the Two and his thirty four thousand friends, who helped Richard to ask for it. Now Art having nothing and no business in this world, the English wanted to make him a saint by piously murdering him at a great feast (with treachery) an old English custom which Art did not like. So, becoming again unreasonable, he left the feast on his horse without saying good bye to the English, and started devastating. Then Richard the Two being twice as vexed, came back again with all his friends to tell Art to stop not wanting to be a saint and being unreasonable, instead of being pleased to have everything taken peacefully by the English, including his life. Whereupon Richard's friends began falling into Art's bogholes covered with grass, and falling over Art's trees in the way, and being frightened by Art in the dark, who was not only Devastating but Harrying.

LAUGHING

So Richard's friends cut down Woods to get at Art and his glasgowglasses who, taking an unfair advantage, would not wait for the woods to be cut down, but galloped off laughing, whereupon the English being now hungry from bogholes, trees, frights in the dark, and Art harrying, rushed into the sea at Wicklow, eating pieces out of ships as they ran. Then Art, calling a meeting, came galloping head downwards on the face of a hill on a horse worth four hundred cows' heads, which when arrived at the meeting place he flung from him with great dexterity, telling the King to go home and mind his own business, being unreasonable all because of the Clam System.

The King going home was disposed, a new King being put up on the throne and Richard throne into prison without the optic,

Downwards

having his eyes put out with red hot irons, also finally beheaded until dead, as was the gentle English custom with Kings disposed.

Meanwhile Art being poisoned while singing an Irish song in O'Doran's Bar, the English considering poison a clean way to make saints, Art and O'Doran both died on the same day, and were also buried, R.I.P. Coming of fine old agricultural stock, their deaths cast a gloom, etc.

THE GERALDINES

These are famous for inventing the G.A.A., including many good hurling and football teams still in a good state of preservation, albeit some of the players being old. They were partly invented by people in fits, viz.: Fitzstephen, Fitzgerald, Fitzmaurice, Fitzburgo, Fitzlacy, Fitzcogan and Fitzarcy, also by Maurice Fitzmaurice Fitzgerald, now also known by Mc-Gillafitzpatrick as the Faithless Norman (see Audrey de Vere). The Geraldines carried out a great Rebellion, which for many reasons was known as the Geraldine Rebellion, but also chiefly for having been thought of by the Geraldines. They also carried it out for many reasons, chiefly being more Norman than the Normans themselves and therefore rebellious, later being more English than the Normans themselves and therefore not being rebellious, also later being more Irish than the Irish themselves and most Irish while still being English in secret, though fighting against the English by a bold stratagem. This was letting on to be rebellows to be loved by all the people now getting used to them.

FOLK LOWER

So they became more Irish than the Irish themselves thus changing from Gulls to Shanagulls respectively, having Irish Stories, bars, cowdoctors, pipers and whitewashers, no hair cuts, marrying women for wives and tissue, and harrying. Their mother the Countess of Desmond not being a nice girl, went stealing apples at 104 years of age, this being unusual for

Sentimentarian

a sentimentarian. Thus she broke her leg falling from an apple tree making her name in history, namely Folk Lower, being taken down from old people, she also being taken down from the apple tree by her mother while saying, 'It is a far far better thing to be or not to be,' this now also being known as The Question.

This did not assist Trade and the Cost of Living went up, the Government watching it closely.

GREAT EARL

The Great Earl was also a Geraldine, being also more Geraldine than the Geraldines themselves. He was also noble, albeit decentrick, having taken up with the young Pretender Lambert Sinwell who pretended to be King of England. Certain places did not like him, however, including Waterford, seeing through him, being the Orbs Infracta, thus causing spectacles, which the King did not like. He had revenge by making the defeated Sinwell Scurrilous in the King's Kitchen, upon which he gave a party or feast (without treachery). The Great Earl seeing Shinwell Scurrilous, did not laugh at the joke, but with a

40

sort of rough simplicity set fire to the Archbishop of Cashel, thinking he was in the Cathedral. This gave rise to his enemies

On Fire

hotly exclaiming while the Archbishop himself was present, 'All Ireland cannot cool this man,' upon which the King with ready wit replied aloud, 'Then let this man fool all Ireland,' thus sending the Great Earl home to fight a bloody battle with the aid of O'Kelly of How Many in the west, thus consorting his position now secure, once more.

POYNING'S LAW

This was so called from the English or Gulls pining away from the inroads of the Irish, who were once more unreasonable. They would not get used to not having their lands, all on account of the Clam system, and they were clamouring to get them back. This vexed the English and made them pass Acts in Privy or counsel with bad provisions. The King sitting in Privy or Counsel, passed an Act to stop the Irish Parliament from passing anything for Ireland until the King passed it first. This law also made it lawful to behead a thief by the neck until dead if found coming or going anywhere, unless he had an English Gull in his company. Thus many Englishmen being beheaded lost their lives from looking more thievish than the

Privy Counsel

Irish themselves, also being thieves coming or going with thieves anywhere under the Act. This gave rise to a great play called the Comedy of Errors by Chaucer, now also noted for bad spelling. From now on the Irish Parliament could not pass anything without the consent of the English King and Privy Counsel, this keeping the Irish Parliament bound, in a way, by England.

NAMES

The King now told the people to take surnames, so that people could call them Mister, also Misses or Miss, thus giving rise to Manners for all the people. The surnames had to be taken from towns such as Sutton, Swords, Newtownmountkennedy and Ballaghderreen, from colours such as Brown, White, Yellow, Heliotrope, Ultramarine blue, and Puce; from trades such as Smith, Taylor, Carpenter, Cook, Sheet-metal-worker, Panel-beater, and Electric Welder; from Hardware, such as Locke, Keyes, Neill, Screw and Gallen; from sore things such as Boyle, Bunyan, Aiken; from virtues such as Keane, Crosse, Savage, Looney; from Golf, such as Green, Devitt; from fish, such as Codd, Roche, Pyke, Ahern; from ships' boats hanging up, such as Davitt, and also other things within the meaning of the Nact or not. Also forbidden was the use of war-cries spoken aloud day or night or in or out or through the medium. This gave rise to the failure of the Act, the Shanagulls now owing to discontent being native squeakers crying without war. The Pale now being harassed, built a double ditch around themselves from sea to sea, also from land to land, the wild war-cries piercing the ditch in various places. These were 'Crumb Aboo' of the great Geraldines of Kildare, so called from the castle of Croom in Limerick, not being Kildare, also 'Shanit Taboo' from the castle of Shanit or Shinat also in Limerick. Well known also for crying in war were the O'Briens, crying the same way as the McCarthys, namely 'Law Flaudher Aboo,' against which no enemy could prevail. 'O'Donnell Boo-Hoo' is the last war cry still preserved in Ireland, not being a war cry

Crying

now however so much as an interval signal, Radio Eireann being now invented, with intervals.

SILKEN THOMAS

Surnamed Sheeda, was son of Garret Oge, son of Garret More, son of Garret Ebhermore, son of Garret Moran More, and was thus well descended in line of male issue. He was fond of style, having two hundred handkerchiefs, then in use in Ireland, also

Fond of Style

other clothes, together with a gorgeous retina of trappings. Yet he was brave, open, generous and young, albeit hot-minded. So when his father, not killing all the people who needed it, had stories about him told to the King, his enemies the Butlers of Ormond being telling on account of being jealous neighbours.

The Ear of the King

Thus the Great Earl was summoned three times for thistles on his land, also tainted for Height Reason, the ear of the King being at the Butlers. So having to go to England to answer charges of cheating also escheating the Kings Avenue, he gave one of his daughters in marriage to O'Connor of Offaly, also one to O'Carroll of Effily to make Himself strong, now ravaging the Butlers and other Gulls and making the Pale paler.

Thereupon having got a peremptory mandate to come at once, he called his son Simple Thomas who was not yet up, and spake a farewell valediction to say in this manner to be wise and well, to be cute with a naked sword of state, also to steer well at the helm of the bark through the waters of his enemies, being many and numerous. He also having now authority was to take sage advice from the Council (without Privy). Thus having spoken his maledictory address, the aged Earl, full of comprehension or fear, departed to the Round Tower of London for the King's Pleasure, leaving Simple Thomas with his retina of seven-score Horsey men to rule in his place.

GRAVE

His enemies now put out, for Simple Thomas to hear, about his father being secretly but piously murdered in the Round Tower of London while waiting to be murdered properly for the King's Pleasure. Simple Thomas being too young to know that the English would not murder his Father nor indeed nobody of that time or now for property, got vexed for nothing. He rushed with his retina to the chamber, not steering calm through the waters of his enemies as said, and flashing his eyes at the Council, threw his naked sword of Office and Ropes of State on the tables, saying 'Take away that empty Bawbee,' this, with tears in the Archbishop's eyes beseeching him not to, being Grave.

SICK

Thereupon his father in the Round Tower of London, waiting to be murdered properly for the King's Pleasure, not being however dead yet, but hearing of Thomas bring havock to his family, took to his bed in the Round Tower and being sick of everything and the Palsy, died, muttering aloud, 'It is a far far better thing to be or not to be,' this being known as the Question. He died also of a broken heart as was the custom, this now being known as Angina Pecteurs, R.I.P., his death

Casting a gloom

having cast a gloom over the Cortege, which testified to the esteem in which all creeds and classes were held in the district, R.I.P.

Simple Thomas with his friends now went out to rise the Lord Drepredy, Lord Leopard Grey, hitting Maynooth Castle in a storm by means of cannon balls out of Canons for the first time in Ireland, whereupon Thomas on condition that his life would be saved now surrendered. The English being pleased, also a polite nation, gave his five uncles a great feast or banquet (with treachery) and to their great surprise firmly hanged them with ropes, with Silken Thomas, at Tieburn for their good. Thomas was now out of clothes also handkerchiefs, which he now did not need albeit having written a letter to O'Brien for them and other clothes, the letter still there. This was the last but final end of the Geraldines, except one born in a basket of clothes at 12 years of age. Thus was founded the Geraldine League for three miles around, to escape the English. And so he did in a basket disgusted as a pheasant to the Continent, though dogged by spies but also fond of dogs, to be later resuscitated

In a basket

and made 11th Earl of Kildare by Mary Queen of Spots. She also was later beheaded by the neck while saying, 'It is a far far better thing to beer or not to beer.' She was also noted for being the cause of bad language, namely Bloody Mary, also unfortunate, having married too often without tissue.

LITERATURE OF THE PERIOD

Literature of the period was very literary, only unhappily all being lost ere written or could be owing to Turmile. This caused decay in Irish Literature by Irishmen, but not in Irish literature by foreign correspondents. Chief of these was Giraldus Cambrensis out of Breakneck in Wales, who was really only Gerald Barry, being partly a Geraldine, coming to Ireland in the Retina of Prince John, sirnamed Blackshanks from the Black Prince winning his Spurs at Agincourt and other places. Giraldibus wrote many articles about Ireland, as is the custom, to give the English true and faithful eye-witness accounts of awful things he saw in Ireland which did not happen. The English people in these strange times were pleased to hear of awful things in Ireland in Eye-witness books by co-respondents from England, whether they happened or not, mostly not. English writers are happily still in a good state of inspiration, notwithstanding Ireland being still hospitable to English co-respondents, who being sharp see things seen by nobody else. this being known as Truth in the News.

HENRY THE EIGHT

Henry, sirnamed Anglia, was a Tudor. He was also, though married, a religious man, being acetic from writing a pious book against Martin Fluther, who had decanted. This gave rise to Henry being Pretender of the Faith, or Fido Defenso, now also known on English coins as Fid. Def. Ind. Imp. Ud. Ense. Gra. Brit. Gram. a Cri. Henry also won his spurs with three feathers couchant or Itch Dien on Cloth of Gold, on Sodden Field 1513, with much pump and sediment, all being carried off however by the Black Debt, which was a plague.

Thus Henry, having all the Cardinal Virtues, invented socks and underwear, and having done so, made Cardigan Wolsey Lord High Chancer and Archbishop of Yolkshire, thus giving rise to the old saying, 'Had I but served my King as should my zeal, he'd jump in the life to come.'

QUEENS

Henry, being noted for Queens, strong feelings, and red beard, had a private life, in which he was always humming 'Haste to the Wedding.' Thus he quickly married Catherine of Araglin,

Haste to the Wedding

who, being left over by his brother by dying, got tired, being without tissue. Henry now had Sir Thomas Moore beheaded by the neck until dead for having composed Moore's Melodies, namely Kate of Araglin, putting Henry in bad humour, thus

46

giving rise to the King now being known affectionately by all the people as Gruff King Hal. His marriage with Catherine now being declared invaluable by Henry, the Pope notwithstanding, also Cardinal Wolsey exclaiming painfully aloud, 'Oh not, Oh not.' Henry having decanted, pushed Catherine aside to press his suit (being neat in dress) on Ann Bowling. Her brother Tom thus becoming a sheer hulk, Henry again decanted, and so incapacited Ann by the neck in a huff. Henry now being lonely married Jane Screymour the day after, marriage now getting to be a habit. Jane dying of tissue, namely Edward the Six, he married with royal dignity Ann of Sleeves, but being up in arms, soon disliked her because of her face which she could not help, thus being innocent. So Henry declaring this marriage nil and void, invented Divorce, a fine old English custom, the English being noted for Chivalry, namely kindness to women.

DISSOLUTION

Henry now dissoluted 3219 monasteries and convents who would not marry, though seeing profuse example of marriage in their royal king. Henry was now affectionately known to all the people as Bluff King Hal, from bluffing Catherine Howard, who thus needlessly married the king, being innocent. Soon with great pomp and splendour he also incapacited Catherine at the neck until dead, she then realising that she had made a mistake, upon which his loyal courtiers buried her alive. Henry was busy in the meantime making himself Lord and King of Ireland, coaxing all the Irish Chiefs by wishing to marry their wives, this being the age of Diplomacy. He also took their lands and houses for his new Knobility who agreed with marriage. Being thus encouraged and too long single, Henry now pressed another suit upon Catherine at Par, she being not related to the disused Catherine of Arragon, also innocent. Catherine at Par unlike her predecessors survived him to the day of his death, without tissue.

Pressing his Suit

CONVENIENT

Henry now having abolished the Pope, invented temporary Wives and a new Religion, all this being Solemnand Convenient. It was thus known as the Deformation, to which everybody now agreed, except 3219 converts and monasteries, the monks and nuns being dissolved because they would not become Deformed. Henry now having done everything he could, and seeing nobody around to marry, also being very married already, laid down his Crown and Spectre, saying, 'I can do no more, let Falstaff do the rest' (see Shakespeare). Thus he piously passed away in the ripe old year of his age from a surfeit of Queens, religion, and the odour of his Sanctity, his final wife Catherine at Par standing by to survive him.

Henry assisted Trade, whereupon the Cost of Living went up.

ELIZABETH

Elizabeth, surnamed Betts, was also a Tudor with leather upholstery. She was noted for many things, including music on the Virginal, an ancient musical instrument with strings, resembling the Spinet, thus becoming known as the Virginal Queen, which amused all the people, they being fond of music. She was also known as Queen of Tarts from a sweet disposition, albeit fickle. Elizabeth, as far as is known, was a daughter of Henry the Eight once removed, of his initial wife but one, Ann Bulleen of Carrick-on-Suir. Her house is now pointed out there to travelling tourists, by local people in a good state of inspiration, thus assisting the Tourist Industry now very important, including good Hotels, also clean Tablecloths for bringing tourists to Ireland to eat good food, the people of Ireland buying bad food from other countries. This was a custom of these lawless times, to Assist Trade.

WATER JUMP

Queen Elizabeth was also noted for Sir Water Raleigh, who was made a Night of by the Queen for jumping a hole of dirty water on a wet day with the Queen in his Sunday coat. The Queen falling backwards into the water, also his Sunday coat, Sir Water exclaimed merrily the while, 'Honi soot qui maly pense,' whereupon Sir Water, observing that the Queen was not amused, set forth at once upon many hazarus voyages for the good of his health and the country. He thus had many hare-breath escapes, being all but drowned in a bucket of

All but drowned

water by his servant while idly inventing cigarettes in the slob
lands of Youghal, now also known as fags. Sir Water thus
escaping, now took to inventing potatoes in the slob lands of
Youghal, namely British Queens to please the Queen. She,
eating the stalks as well, being hungry, got very vexed, thus
sending for Raleigh, saying she wished to incapactitate him at
the neck, whereupon he, observing that the Queen was not
amused, set forth at once upon many hazarous voyages for the
good of his health, sea air even then being usefel, being full of
benzone.

GOOD QUEEN

Sir Water now planting, as was the old English Custom in
Ireland, namely 47,000 acres of Irish Queens on his lawn at
Youghal, thus caused a famine, not feeding the Irish in the
bogholes, their lands being taken, as was the custom, by force
of peaceful penetration, also Martial Aid under many beneficial
Acts, including Scutage, Grabbage, and Holdage of the Frugal
System. This kindness of the Queen in wanting to feed hungry
Irish living in Bogholes (but not succeeding) now gave rise to
her being known as Good Queen Bess, also to many songs in
her honour, including allegory songs, namely, 'The Garden
where the Praties Grow.' The Queen is thus famed in song for
a Grecian bent to walk right through the world as Nature did
intend, wearing a French dress. The Queen now being pleased
to be thought good by all the people, once more fell secretly in
love with Sir Water Raleigh, and so once more had him fondly
cast into her favourite dungeon, he not having time to go on
many hazarous voyages (see etc.). He now wiled away the
time by writing allegory on the walls in the dark dungeon,
namely, 'Fain would I climb but that I fear to fall.' The Queen
hearing this was at last amused. 'Let the boy win his spuds,'
she said, and sentenced the noble Courtier to have his i put out
(all Elizabeth's Courters having their i put out), also to be
executed for fifteen years, muttering strongly in his beer with
his dying breath, 'O tempora, Oh Mores, Oh fugit, Oh Queen

49

of Tarts!' The fifteen years being up, it being spent in writing history, he was justly executed by James the First, fifteen years too late. James the First is so called, however, from being the first to execute him. Writing history is not useful.

FOWL

The Queen now wanting to rule the waves, her hair beings straight, took to fowl means, namely Admirable Drake on the High Seize striking fear into the heart of the Spanish Armada, including 35,000 veterates under the Duke of Parma Violets. This was however really due to bad weather, the English pretending to burn the Spanish King's beard, the Spanish King

Admirable Drake

really being shaved. Nevertheless, the good Queen Bess had a glorious rein, it being good for the potatoes in Ireland, thus assisting Trade, the Cost of Living also going up, the Queen keeping nothing down. The Queen also tried to hold Deformation in Ireland, telling the people to read the Book of Comic Prayer, which they did not do, being unreasonable, upon which the Queen being pious, told all the people in Ireland to go to Church or Hell, which they being stubborn, would not. This was the Act of Informity, passed in good faith by the Queen.

PLANTATION

The first Plantation in Ireland was that of Leeks and Offaly, the English planting dragon's teeth which was pulled up by armed men. This was due to the Irish being now too plentiful in spite of the English having tried to reduce them by powerful weapons, namely Force and Diplomacy, still in use down to modern times, albeit much improved. The Irish being still there in spite of force, namely bloody Force of bloody Arms, the kind English often getting hurt in using it, the English now tried Diplomacy, not being so hard on the health, the English being careful of their health. This was to coax the Irish to go away out of their homes and lands and die, which they would not do, not having a proper spirit of co-operation, now also to be found in creameries and Denmark. So it now being the Springtime of the year, the time was ripe for Planting, namely to tell the Irish to go away out of their homes and lands and live in bogholes, thus making room for nice English people who would always do what they were told, being well brought up, namely the Old School Toy. But the Irish not having the good will to solve the difficulty of the English wanting their homes, would not go, whereupon the soldiers came to endeavour to make them see reason. This took up the time of the soldiers from going away to protect other small nations, as was the English custom, the Irish refusing to lay the foundations for a satisfactory settlement of this complex problem, thus endangering world peace. This was a disappointment to Queen Mary of Maryborough, now dying of a broken heart with 'Cabbage' printed on it, as she said it would be through not being able to plant, and not, as other historians say, to six Bruisers from Calais, with keys.

PLANTATION OF MUNSTER

The Plantation of Munster was so called from being a Plantation, the Geraldines now being liquidated and the weather also wet. The land of Munster now being waste, the lowing of a ploughman or the whistle of a cow train could not be heard in all the fairs of Ireland. Thus was 'a most plentifull countrie suddainley left voide of man and beaste, the people creeping forth upon their hands from the woods and glynnes, for their legges would not bear them, so that any stony hart would have rued the same.' Thus the people being too weak to spell properly, also ignorant, the time was ripe to give their land to nice people with accents from England, willing to come over here, also able to spell.

The Land Commission now became very active, as is its custom, dividing land night and day, giving a large farm to Sir Water Raleigh, this not being due, however, to his having a cousin in the Department. Sir Water now going on no more hazarus voyages for the good of his health and his country, planted 47 thousand acres of bad potatoes on his lawn at Youghal, this now being known as Black 47. Sir Water is very good for tourists, from leaving his house at Youghal still for visitors, also his potatoes.

Edmund Spenser also out of England, now received the rest of Munster, this however, not being due also to his having a cousin in the Land Commission, but to fair play, for which the English are always very noted. Spenser, however, was not a good farmer either, being too fond of social life, thus passing his time eating Irish babies in Kilcolman Castle, also dancing with Faerie Queens in all the forts of Ireland. This was the cause of Spenser now turning into a poet, also giving way to bad spelling, picked up from the ignorant Irish, nevertheless becoming famous, being now praised by all the people not having read his poetry.

Thus was Munster planted. Cousins are useful.

Cousins are useful

GERALDINE REBELLION

The Geraldines carried out their great Rebellion through living in Kildare, the seat of the Curragh and soldiers, also many race horses and wall paper, encouraging home industry, the rebellion being held in Desmond's Green valleys look down on thy love. It was carried out by Gerald FitzGarret Fitzgerald, but not

Laying Waste

fully, he being incarcerated in the Tour of London together with his brother who was innocent, James FitzMaurice Fitz-

Garret FitzGerald, who could not carry it out. It was thus left to his cousin but one, Garret FitzMaurice Fitzgarret Fitzgerald, to the dismay of Fitzbutler of Ormond, then meeting in secret to make an unholy pact, thus forcing the noble Fitzstephen Fitzjames Fitzgerald into open and secret revolt against the English. So he flew from Shannon to Spain to seek for help. Coming back he laid waste until sorely slane in a bog at Skirmush by Barrington's Bridge. His place at the head of his family was bravely taken by John Fitzmaurice Fitzhenry Fitzgerald, who soon died from disinterry from having no cabbage, in the wood of Claoughlaoiss, his place being taken by Thomas Fitzgarret Fitzmaurice Fitzgerald, in line with his cousin but one.

NETTLES

He while laying waste was captured in a hovel near Tralee, once living in a river up to his neck all night with his Countess. He said to the Soldiers, 'Spare my life,' but the soldiers, not being economical, would not spare anything. Thus at one fell blow he was entirely decapitated by the neck until dead, his head with great prudence (after a post-mortem) being salted in a box and sent to the Queen. She being pleased to receive such

In a box

a trophy, it being grisly notwithstanding, thus made at once her Lord Depredy in Ireland a Night of the Queen's Garter. This assisted trade, and the Cost of Living went up. Thus ended the great Geraldine Rebellion, carried out by the Geraldines who were completely Exterminated, there being however other Geraldines of which more anonymous, living secret lives until the lowing of a ploughshare or the whistle of a cow could not be heard in all the fairs of Ireland from Cashel to Dundrum in the West. This is stated by the Sore Masters in their now famous Annuals, also full of other history, thus giving rise once more to the old saying. 'To every cow its low and to every plough its whistle.' The people now came crawling through the ditches with nettles in their mouths, this being due to lying Waist, also no cabbage or any other vegetables, thus giving Dissentery to all the people. This did not assist Trade and the country did not go ahead greatly, the Government however saying it did, and the Cost of Living went up. This was not a nice rebellion, being mixed, therefore not easy to remember, not being clear, the student of history thus getting no marks.

RED HUGH

Shane O'Neill, Simple Thomas and other people now being over, the time was ripe for Red Hugh, not however a Communist, he only getting red when thinking of the English. He was also known as Hugh Rue from having rued going to an English Party (with treachery;).

This noble lad was son of the proud chieftain of Tirconnell. While being a boy to pass his youth away, he was famed throughout the length and breadth of the land for wisdom beyond his tender ears. The English hearing this did not like it, knowing that when young Red Hugh grew up into a chieftain he would be unreasonable, also nobody had any right to be famous but the English.

IRON FEATURES

The young Aedh Ruadh (pron. Air Ugh, to assist foreign speakers, not native like us natives) was living with his foster-father McSwilly of the Battleaxes on the shores of Rathmullen. The English Lord Depredy, Long John Parrot, sent a ship to Rathmullen, a plot being hatched to get Red Hugh under hatches. The plot being a success through young Red Hugh accepting a kind English invitation to a ship's party (with treachery), the ship sailed off to Dublin. Young Hugh, a prisoner was now not merely put but thrown into Dublin Castle, a cruel and bloody place, being noted for Income Tax. His arms now being removed the English put iron features on his feet, also chained him to the wall.

Hatching a plot

FILES

Red Hugh now being a groan man in the Dungeons of Dublin Castle, 'having spent four years eating out his heart,' the food being bad, found a file in his plum pudding on Christmas Day. Strange things are still found in plum puddings in modern times, also in Dublin Castle in files of Income Tax. So Red Hugh filing away the time in his dungeon by filing the features off his feet, let himself down mainly by a rope into the sewerage of Dublin, thus escaping. Sewerage is now also useful to many Irish writers to let themselves down, this now being known as Escapism from Red Hugh escaping, also as Art, to make books sell. The English being a cultured nation have good taste in sewerage, also using it in most books to sell, this being known as holding the mirror up to nature, namely Realism, which is mostly stark.

BIG TOES

Red Hugh and his companions not having a merry Christmas owing to snow, the plum pudding also being left behind, now walked through the streets to a rock in the mountains of Wicklow. Their shoes full of sleet and with sleet in their shirts they lay on the sleet on the rock, thus almost perishing. They were however recovered by Fiach McHugh McByrne, who

Found a File

being a well-known firebrand, melted the snow, all except Hugh's big toes, which owing to freezing had to be cut off from the neck until dead. They were then salted in a box to be hung up on the battlemen in Dublin Castle, to strike terror into all other Irish Malafoosters. They were not, however, sent to the Queen, who did not like big toes, much preferring salted heads in a box, this being due to English Culture.

HUMAN CRY

The human cry was now raised throughout the land for Red Hugh, the English wanting him back. Despite this, Red Hugh, secretly riding a horse under the saddle, slipped through the enemy watchdogs to the north, where he was exclaimed by all the people. He now spent twelve months in bed, being sick of the English; and being unreasonable, he recovered. His feeble father now throwing up, Red Hugh was made chief of Tirconnell, standing on the ancient rock of the O'Donnells with

Slipped Through

all the ancient rites (except big toes). This vexed the English thus giving rise to all the English saying 'O'Donnell Taboo' (see Radio Eireann).

ANOTHER HUE

Hugh O'Neill being another Hugh, also able, was noted for building a house with bullets at Dungannon, also for being son of Matt the Dark the son of Conn the Bockock. Hugh was well educated by the Queen to make him English, the English being noted for education, being superior, this being due to the old school toy, not yet worn out. Hugh was in great favour at the Queen's Court, nevertheless although having wormed his way into the Queen's heart, Hugh, unlike the Queen's Kidney, was not the Queen's anything.

PROBLEM

Hugh having become almost an English gentleman, namely an officer in the Queen's Army, was now sent to Ireland to hold Ulster for the Queen, the English even then being fond of Ulster. Hugh also was to civilise the Irish, thus helping to bring about a better understanding between the sister nations. This was a complex problem of a peculiar nature, bristling with difficulties, as is the way with English problems down to modern times. It was not however so difficult that it could not be solved with patience and good will, also with a proper realisation of the issues involved, namely to give it to the English.

Hugh now seeing what English rule in Ireland was like, changed his mind, thinking instead to civilise the English, not telling the English his mind, however, not being noted for honour. This was from having no tie in England, preferring Irish poplin.

Whereupon now being more Irish than his uncle Shane himself, Hugh roofed his house with bullets to keep out the English. He also put his men in drills by moonlight in lonely places, now thinking to advise the English, by means of guns, to solve their complex problem by getting out of Ireland and going back to their own country. In this noble endeavour he was helped by Red Hugh, whose sister he married, brothers-in-law in these strange times, sometimes helping each other.

STOLEN

Hugh's wife having sadly died, thus casting a gloom, Hugh now got married to Mabel Bagsenal, a nice girl, albeit a sister of Marshal Bagsenal, in spite of him. Marshal, although descended (a long way) from the Firbolgs or Bagsmen, did not like his brother-in-law so he furiously stole Mabel's fortune, maybe twelve thousand pounds of our money if we had money, the Cost of Living going up, the Government just gone, however, being always to blame for this and everything.

PARTS

The Queen now being furious, gathered an army to fight a bloody battle, telling her men to liquidate O'Neill by all lillimigette means, and send his head salted in a box. A new Depredy, Lord Borough of Rabbit, was sent over to persecute the war. He being a good general, had a clever plan, namely dividing his army into three equal halves. These were Gulls under Sir Concrete Clifford (a kind man, albeit over here killing people) to go up and liquidate O'Donnell on the left-hand side; Shanagulls under young Bargainstill, son of Lord Trimblestill, to liquidate in the middle; and the Lord Depredy himself to go liquidating on the right.

NOUGHT

But the plan came to nought due to O'Neill, not playing the game by also making up a plan. Thus Sir Concrete, albeit being reinforced, was liquidated by O'Donnell with his army and grief in the Curlews (pron. Coorloons). Young Bargainstill was liquidated in the middle and the Drepedy was liquidated by O'Neill on the Blackwater, the three English armies being all wet. Everybody (who was not liquidated) was sorry for Sir Concrete, being a kind man, his sudden and untimely death in battle almost casting a gloom, etc.

YELLOW

The Queen now being twice as furious, gathered another army to fight under Marshal Bagsenal in the van to kill O'Neill for good. O'Neill, however, forgetting his good English education, namely that might is right, put brambles in the pits to knock the horses (potato pits having been invented by Sir Water Raleigh while he was alive). Thus fell the gallant Bagsenal into a pit with a cannon ball embedded in his brain, whereupon he evacuated. Colonel Crossby taking over to no effect, also evacuated the field of battle, also Molaire O'Reilly, the Queen's O'Reilly, exclaiming, 'Change Queens with me and I'll never fight again,' which he never did, dying suddenly owing to O'Neill not being the Queen's Hugh nor the Queen's Anything.

Thus was won the Battle of the Yellow Foe, from the English being yellow, evacuating from having nobody else to fight their battle, as is the custom in modern times, this being due to Diplomacy (see U.S.A.).

INSECTS

The Queen now being three times as furious, gathered an army to fight a bloody battle under her favoured Courtier Essex (a nice man) to blot out O'Neill by all illegible means. Essex, however, was distracted by Insects, also the Irish not playing the game, took down the signposts. This made Essex go to

Turned South

search for the rebellion where it was not. Not being fond of rebellions either, being better as a Courtier, he led his sixteen thousand infantile troops and thirteen hundred calvary to winter in the South for the Summer, thus with great military foresight keeping away from O'Neill. He was not in good luck, however, his rear being shattered by Owney O'Moore at the Pass of the Plums, so called from the fruits of victory going to the Irish, the English also having their features scattered from out their helmets all over the plain.

The Queen now being four times as furious, told Essex to come home, to be put to the sore on the block. The future story of this unlucky Courtier belongs to English history, having no place in the Irish Chronicological of these lawless times, when the blowing of a ploughman or the whistle of a train could not be heard from Dunqueen to the West.

JOLLY

The Queen now being five times as furious, gathered an army to fight a bloody battle under Mountjoy, so called from being a jolly man, he having Sir George Carew, Lord Precipice of Munster, another jolly man, to help him. These two gallant English soldiers went bravely forth to fight the crops, sending soldiers with sickles, scythes, crowbars, forks, penknives, and thistle-cutters to tear up the corn and burn the houses and other crops. This the brave soldiers bravely did, leaving the fair cultivated land a smiling black ruin, and the people to crawl out of the ditches without legges, with nothing but nettles in their mouths, thereupon Mountjoy and his brave army returned to Dublin singing, 'Play up, play up and play the game.' This was to bring about a better understanding between the two nations, an old custom of the English in countries taken by them to be protected, the English being a nation famous for Protection.

SURROUNDED

The Spanish Fleet now having entered Kinsale Harbour with Don Juan Del Ah Agilla in command, he took Kinsale. Whereupon the Queen, now being six times as furious, this being the Divine Rite of Queens, told Mountjoy to go down with his army and hunt the Spanish. Mountjoy (albeit preferring fighting against the crops) came around Kinsale, surrounding it completely, but on one side only, whereupon his men began to die of descentery from no cabbage (having rooted it all), also of famine in profusion, also of broken heart as was the custom. O'Neill now completely surrounded Mountjoy on one side and O'Donnell on the other, with the Spanish solidly entrenched in his rear, his unfortunate rear, like that of Essex, being unprotected.

Unfortunate rear

DARK

O'Neill now wanted to let the English die of descentry in peace but Red Hue O'Donnell, getting red from thinking of his big toes, wanted them to die in pieces. Thus Mountjoy was now in sore straights from being surrounded inside and outside, his rear being harassed by the Spanish. Nevertheless, the Irish going astray in the dark by means of a traitor, were attacked by Mountjoy in the dark without being ready. Ah Agilla did not come out as promised, it being too early in the morning before the breakfast, also he having a sore heel from tight boots. Thus was lost the battle of Kinsale. Don Juan Del Ah Agilla then surrendered the town and went home. The Spanish King Philip of Spain, shaking his finger sadly at him, murmured, 'Ah, Agilla,' upon which Agilla died of a broken heart, being very touchy, R.I.P., his untimely demise however casting no gloom in Ireland.

POPULAR

Thus was lost the historic battle of Kinsale, now also well known to be a very historic battle, mainly through changing the whole course of Irish history if it had not been lost. It was, however, lost through the Irish being out all night in the dark without their arms, the E.S.B. not yet having been invented. This is a plan to make light out of water, now a blessing to rural places not in towns or cities, the climate of Ireland being also damp.

Thus the Irish lost through wanting to fight when they should not, also not being ready to fight when they should, also from bad surroundings, also the English liking the dark, not nowadays however being trusted in the dark, the sun never setting upon their dominions.

Kinsale is now, however, a popular battle from being easy to remember, thus being good for marks (see Clontawf).

Whereupon O'Donnell, going to Spain, died from a surfeit of English poison, for a joke. O'Neill going to Rome, died there of much Honour, both deaths casting a gloom, R.I.P.

PLANTATION OF ULSTER

The Earls being gone off to Rome to die holy but natural deaths, this not being possible in Ireland, the people of Ulster now became very indolent, not even burying the dead, thus it became necessary to plant them. This was done by English Undertakers, whose duty it was to take the land and bury the ignorant Irish, who would not bury themselves. But this Plantation was also a failure, the narrow-minded Ulster people, not having learned Co-operation, now also useful in creameries, refusing to die or be buried. Instead they went off into bogholes in a sulk, from which they fiercely issued forth, killing all the Undertakers when they were not looking, thus making it difficult for the Undertakers to bury anybody, not even themselves.

This Plantation was the cause of much history including Orangemen and Orangewomen. The Sash me Father Wore, a Protestant Parliament for a Protestant People, No Popery, No Catholics, No Bigotry, and other noble sentiments. This gave rise to Ulster being loyal, always wanting to be conscripted to fight England's battles, it being braver to be conscripted than to go themselves, this causing them to stay at home. History is not useful.

DIVINE RIGHT

Charles the Once (sirnamed Stuart) a handsome man, although of Scotch distration, now became King of England. He displeased the Rum Parliament by wanting to do things himself, not knowing that an English King can do nothing, except look pleased; being kept only for show (even if ugly), also for all the people to put his coloured picture in the parlour and sing God Save him.

Charles also got married to the wrong girl, thus vexing the Rum Parliament without their consent, English Kings never

Wrong Girl

being allowed to marry the girl they like, this being known as the Divine Right of Kings. He also kept the old Catholic religion, which would not let people change their wives before they were dead. Thus all the people said the king was wrong, everybody but the English people being wrong, including their first wives if alive.

GREASES

Charles now being short of money, an old custom with married men, also having a greasy palm, invented the Greases, to sell to the Irish people for one hundred and twenty thousand pounds (not of our money). The Irish, thinking the Greases were real instead of promises, gave Charles the money.

Charles now being again short of money (the Cost of Living having gone up) sent Sir Thomas Wentforth (surnamed Strafford) to Ireland to collect more money, collections in Ireland being an old custom (still in a good state of preservation). Strafford having invented Taxation, namely getting money for nothing, now also invented Irish linen, having abolished Irish wool. Now going back to England, Strafford was declared a peach by the Rum Parliament, and abolished, namely sundrily beheaded.

The King now also being impeached was also abolished. 'He nothing common did nor mean upon the memorable scene, but with his Keener eye the axe's edge did try,' saying with royal dignity to his executioner, who was worried, 'This is my headache.' The Executioner thus relieved, now swung his murderous axe, remarking as he did so, 'Bonnie Charlies noo awa'. Whereupon all the people, standing to attention, sang, 'God Save Our King' with hats off out of respect, the English people always being very devoted to the Royal family, this now being known as English Loyalty.

The Grease Lend of the King was a failure, for the Irish.

God Save Our King

REBELLION OF 1641

This was so called from being held in 1641 and other places for long after, also called the War of the Revolution from not being a proper war owing to people revolting from one side to another. Thus, it had to be divided into four large parts, namely Old Irish, Middle Irish, New Irish, Old English, Young English, Catholics, Prodestants, Pretenders, Contenders, Extenders, Pressbetarians, Puritarians, Parliamentarians, Royalists, Loyalists, Cavileers, Roundheads, Fatheads, Sickheads, Considerates, Nonconsiderates, Nonconformists, Noncomposmentis, Noncompoops, Regicides, Parricides, Covenanters, Recusants, Concussants, Prestons, Munros, Ormonds, etc.

MIXED

This was a mixed rebellion being partly carried out to unplant the Plantation of Ulster, also partly to let the Catholics stay Catholics, the English wanting the Deformation with exchange of wives, people with plenty of wives being soon easy to govern. The rebellion was partly carried out by Sir Phelim O'Neill, feeling his way into Ulster with pitchforks, hay-knives, razorblades and gateposts, also by Rory O'Fore in Leinster (see Cathleen Ban). This rebellion ruined all the history books, however, by being mixed, thus causing the Confabulation of Kilkenny to unmix it, namely to explain to all the people who was fighting who and for why or for what purpose.

Thus the Confabulation, wishing to carry out the rebellion properly, sent to Spain for Owen Roe O'Neill, being a great soldier, to tell him to put the four parts of the Army in rows properly. O'Neill being a good General though not English, now took an unfair advantage, putting his army between two hills on a fine day, also dividing it into seven halves, with three halves to fill the gaps between four halves, also a wood at his rear, this being known as Strategy.

SUNSHINE

Munro being tired from marching, could not fight properly, this being a good excuse. The sun was also in his eyes (sunglasses being scarce owing to the war) this being another good excuse, thus making Munro and his army want to go home, the English preferring the dark, the English also always having good excuses.

But O'Neill not playing the game, told his soldiers to go and kill a lot of the English soldiers, which they did, thus causing a fierce battle. The English, being tired, thus lost the battle, also Munro's wig, all because of the sun shining into their faces out of O'Neil's rear. So was lost the Battle of Benblurb, also Munro's wig through sunshine, not through dark, as at Kinsale, Munro's wig remaining on the green.

FIRE

The next important thing to happen was Lord Inchaquinch, so called from his habit of quenching fires, also being known as Murrogh of the Turnings, from his habit of turning from side to side. He is now also noted for lighting a pastoral fire with people in it, in the Cathedral of Cashel, upon which

Quenching

ended the people, the Cathedral, also the Rebellion of 1641, the fair land of Ireland being reduced to a smiling black ruin, with the people once more without legges in the ditches, sucking nettles. Thus was ended a difficult rebellion for the student, not being held properly, therefore not good for marks.

WART

Odliver Cromwell (pron. Corsa Crummell) was loved by all the people, being a brewer. He was also a great Englishman from being stern and gloomy, also from having a big Wart upon his nose, underneath which were deep religious feelings. This gave rise to Puritarians, who were noted for piety, being born with a Bible in one hand and a Sore in another. They were also known as Roundheads, from their heads always turning round, looking for somebody to butcher.

Religious Feelings Underneath

NAMES

Codliver Cromwell the Puritan leader, now being too pious for a brewer, thus turned butcher to the King; and having butchered the King, the people hailed him, crying aloud, 'Thou wart the Lord Protectus.' Thus Cromwell, by popular exclamation, became the Lord Protectus of the Commonwelt, his followers also having long and holy names, namely Praise-God-Bare-bones, Good-God-Squint-Eyes, Lord-God-Scratch-My-Back, Great-God-Bust-Em-All, etc. etc.

IRON

These Puritarians being pious, were now against everything, including the Cavileers, who were against nothing, being gentlemen with hair and long horses. So Cromwell getting vexed, rushed into the Rum Parliament with a naked sore and several others in his rear, shouting aloud, 'Take away them

Gawbees,' upon which the Gawbees took themselves away. Thus ended the Rum Parliament, which had sat so long, a soldier named Praise-God-Barebones throwing the Maze, which was the cymbal of authority, down into the backyard. Thus Cromwell's soldiers now became known as Cromwell's Iron-works, the Maze being made of iron.

CURE

Cromwell now turned his face (with wart) towards Ireland, to bring about a better understanding between the sister nations. Ireland was also famous for cures for warts, namely a snail rubbed in to it upon a thorn, also a fasting spit rubbed in to it three times daily after breakfast. The people of Drogheda, being sorry for Cromwell gave him these cures.

CHIVALRY

Cromwell's wart, however, not being cured, by reason of his having no spit, also the snails hurrying away on seeing him coming, Cromwell was not pleased. So looking into his mirror not once but many times, he told his butchers to put their Bibles in one hand and their sores in another, also their meat saws, which they did. Then Cromwell told them to go out and butcher all the people, women and children first, Cromwell being full of Chivalry, albeit being only a farmer's son from Huntingdon, now also noted for other things. Wereupon Cromwell's Ironspikes doing as said, butchered all the people, except some nervous citizens who, taking alarm, ran away, crying 'The Lord Protectus.' Nevertheless three thousand citizens died in the odour of sanctity from Cromwell and his butchers.

NO CURE

Cromwell now hearing of good cures in Wexford' namely to put a stone as big as the wart, having rubbed the wart upon it, into a bag, to be put at a crossroads, to be found by a man to take the wart. So Cromwell hurried to Wexford, the people sending messengers the length and breadth of the land to find a stone as big as Cromwell's wart, also a bag big enough to hold the stone, also a crossroads big enough to put the bag at, also a man with a nose big enough to hold the wart. This is now all well known as Folk Lower, being collected with machines out of old people nearly dead, including songs and Shanuckles.

BLOODY

The messengers having now returned, not finding nor Stone nor bag nor crossroads nor man in all the land big enough for Cromwell's wart, Cromwell, looking in his mirror not once but many times, was more displeased. Therefore he told his iron soldiers to massage the people of Wexford, women and children first. This they did with Bibles, sores, and meat saws, in a cruel and bloody massage. The children now left in Ireland were sent off to the Barbarous Islands in the West, to learn Irish.

BREECHES

Hugh Dubh now at Clonmel, 'was the stoutest enemy Cromwell's army ever met with,' many of the Roundheads being fat too. Cromwell and his soldiers coming to the wall, soon made large breeches to get in. Hugh Dubh and his brave soldiers, attacking them from all sides, drove Cromwell and his men out of their breeches, thus two thousand of Cromwell's soldiers pe-

Out of their breeches

rished, the weather being severe. Hugh and his men now being out of bullets (lead being scare owing to the war), went off to Waterford, thus Cromwell took Clonmel, it not being a famous victory.

SEDIMENT

Ireland was now at peace, Cromwell having butchered all the people, also given their lands to his butchers for their cattle. The butchers, however, kindly said, 'To Hell with Connacht,' thus nobly refusing to take any lands, except those of Ulster, Leinster, and Munster. Whereupon the Irish people crossed the Shannon on the 25th of May, and went to Hell in Connacht. Thus was brought about the Great House, Hunt Balls, County Clubs, Demesnes, Manors, Landlords, Squireens, Shoneens, Gombeens, mud cabins, pigs in the parlour, Bedad, Bejabers, Begorrah and other well-known features of Irish life, being more Irish than the Irish themselves. This is now well known as the Cromwellian Sediment, still in a good state of preservation.

It is not known where Cromwell went to when he died. He did not got to Connacht.

Appendix III

(From the *Drogheda Weekly Courier*, Saturday, September 12th, 1649.)

MR. CROMWELL AT DROGHEDA

Mr. Oliver Cromwell, the well-known liquidator, who is now touring Ireland for the first time, was the guest of honour at a banquet given for him by the Mayor and Corporation at the Town Hall, Drogheda, on Wednesday night.

The Mayor, in extending a hearty cead mile failte to Mr. Cromwell, said that the fame of his deeds had preceded him, and that his name was well-known and likely to be long remembered, not merely in Ireland, but by all liberty-loving peoples. He also apoligised to Mr. Cromwell for the absence of some 3,000 citizens who had been unavoidably detained, and he sincerely hoped that Mr. Cromwell would enjoy his tour, and bring back with him many pleasant memories of his contacts with the Irish people.

Mr. Cromwell, in a felicitous speech of reply, said:—
'Mr. Mayor, Ladies and Gentlemen,

It give me—hic—great pleasure to address you 'ere to-night in this—hic—'istoric city of Drog'eda. I am very 'appy to be amongst you—in fact—hic—your steaks and your—hic—whiskey are so good that at this—hic—moment I am 'appy to be anywhere—hic—I am just—hic—'appy—just—hic—'appy.

Though I ave been but a—hic—short time in your—hic—beautiful country, I 'ave been studying your mel—hic—odious language, and I can now say—hic—"Law bree" and—hic—'Deese merra gut" as well as the—hic—best of you (*hear, hear*). Although this is my first—hic—visit, I sincerely 'ope it will not be my—hic—last. In fact, I do not feel a stranger at all, for I 'ave—hic—studied the—hic—'istory of your—hic—'istoric land, a—hic—'istory of unceasing struggle against injustice and hoppression. I am, Ladies and Gentlemen, but a mere—hic—Henglishman, but I am, I—hic—'ope, like every true—hic—Henglishman, a lover of liberty—liberty in the—hic—widest—hic—sense, of that much-abused word. You—hic—Hirish resemble us Henglish. I 'ope nobody will be offended at my—hic—saying so (*no, no*). You Hirish, I—hic—say, resemble us Henglish in your—hic—fine determination, your defiance of bad—hic—Governments, and your—hic—sympathy with hoppressed peoples the—hic—world hover (*hear, hear*).

I am, therefore, proud to have set my foot on the—hic—soil of your storied country, 'allowed by the—hic—blood of hinnumerable martyrs. The magic of your hincomparable land has captivated my—hic—'eart; this is indeed a land worth fighting for, if one could be so—hic—brutal as to fight. I may be misunderstood—Henglishmen in Hireland sometimes are (*no, no*)—but I do not—hic—mind saying that it 'as often been to me a hoccasion of hacute distress that the moment the very—hic—name of Hireland is mentioned, many of my—hic—countrymen seem to bid hadieu to common feeling, common prudence and common sense, and to hact—hic—with the barbarity of tyrants and the fatuity of hidiots (*groans*).

My 'eartfelt hadmiration 'as been reserved for your struggle against those who would—hic—deprive you of your hancient faith. I blush, Ladies and Gentlemen, for my—hic—countrymen's be'aviour in the past—I deplore the misguided policy which would—hic—deprive you of your priceless 'eritage. Bigotry is a —hic—festering sore which heats deep into the 'eart of the body politic (*hear, hear*). My countrymen should 'ave caused several Papists—I mean Catholics, to be dissected —after death, I mean, by—hic—surgeons of either religion, and the report to be published with—hic—haccompanying plates. If the viscera and other horgans of life 'ad been found to be the same as in Puritan bodies; if the provisions of—hic—nerves, harteries, cerebrum and cerebellum 'ad been the same as we are provided with, or as the Puritans are now known to possess, then indeed they might—hic—'ave convinced my country at large of the strong probability that the—hic—Papists—I mean Catholics—are really 'uman creatures, hendowed with the feelings of men and hentitled to all their rights (*prolonged applause*).

I 'ope I 'ave said enough (*yes, yes*). I 'ope I 'ave said enough, my Hirish friends—I 'ope I may now—hic—call you friends (*yes, yes*) to show that I respect your—hic—religious beliefs, and the inalien—the—hic—inalienable rights—temporal rights—of the people of Hireland. Too long 'ave the—hic—sister nations been separated by mis—hic—misunderstanding. The brutal weapon of war must be outlawed. World peace must depend on—hic—mutual charity and mutual compre'ension and therefore I say—hic—that w'at we in Hengland desire in our relations with this—hic—'istoric nation —the policy that we desire to see carried out must, if it is—hic —to be—to be—to be successful, depend in the—hic—long run on mutual good will and mutual—hic—bunderstanding (*loud* applause).

Everything which makes for the greatness of the Hirish papists—I mean people—I will—hic—support. Everything which tends to lower the—hic—Hirish people I will oppose. The masses must be huplifted and heducated and the—hic—the —hic—drift from the land must—hic—be checked. There are great possibilities—possibilities—great possibilities for—hic— Ireland under Henglish guidance and we Henglish are always prepared to place our—hic—ability to govern at your—hic— disposal, so that you may in time attain to the—hic—Henglish love of self-respec which is the henvy of the 'ole world (a voice, "Sez you!").

The interrupter having had his head removed, Mr. Cromwell went on:—

"Justice, Ladies and Gentlemen, must be done—justice that plays no favourites and knows no standards but the hequal rights of the two nations concerned; and no special or separate hinterest of one—hic—nation can be made the basis of any settlement w'ich is not consistent with the common hinterest of Both. I thank you Mr.—hic—Mayor, Ladies and Gentlemen, for your kind--hic--reception 'ere to-night and for your lovely w'iskey, w'ich 'as made me very 'appy—so 'appy, kind friends, that I—hic—'ardly know w'at I'm saying (*loud applause*). In fact I am thinking in future, my—hic—friends, of practising my—hic—profession with the—hic—Bible in one 'and and a— hic—double w'iskey in the other (*laughter*).

Mr. Cromwell then signed the Roll of Freemen of the City, after which he was presented with a keg of poteen, also addresses from the Town Planning Committee, the Land Settlement Committee, the Society of St. Vincent de Paul, and the Society for The Prevention of Cruelty to Anybody. In reply to these, Mr. Cromwell, who was much moved, said:

"My friends, for I now feel—hic—that I am among friends (*yes, yes*), I thank you from the—hic—bottom of my 'eart. I am in full—hic—very full agreement with the aims and hobjects of your—hic—charitable societies. I am old-fashioned enough—hic—to believe—hic—that kind 'earts are more than coroners. For, as you already know, great is charity and—hic

—stronger than all things. If I may—hic—be permitted to—hic—quote from a Puritan document like the Bible (*yes, yes*). "Charity doeth the things that are just, and—hic—refraineth from all unjust and wicked things, and all men do well like of her works! I thank you, Ladies and Gentlemen, and it—hic—gives me—hic—great pleasure to subscribe to your—hic—charitable societies my—hic—'eartiest wishes for their success.'

Mr. Cromwell then took the opportunity to apologise to the charitable societies for any extra burdens which might be thrown upon them by any thoughtless outbursts of exuberance on the part of his party, and which might have caused inconvenience to some of the citizens. As Mr. Cromwell put it, one cannot 'ave a homelette without someone getting 'urt,' but he assured the citizens who were still alive that such incidents would not occur again.

Mr. Cromwell and his party then left by road for Wexford, where, it is understood, a reception is being prepared for them.

Settled

Charles The Two (surnamed the Unjust Stuart), being son of Charles The One on his mother's side, was noted for many things, also noted for being noted, thus giving rise to him being called The Merrie Monarch by all the people. Charles, albeit being of Scotch distraction, was a promising man like his father, rewarding the faithful Irish who fought for him with rich promises. He also passed an Act of Settlement (written in Irish

Merrie Monarch

to make people like it) to settle the English Settlers in the Irish settlements in which they had been settled by unsettling the

71

Irish. This was followed by an Act of Explanation (in English so that the people could read it, as is now the custom) to explain to the unsettled Irish why the missettled English missettlers should be settled in the Irish dissettlement in which they were mis-settled, not being asked to explain.

PASSED

Charles The Two also passing his time when not being merrie, in passing Acts not in Privy Council but openly, also passed many other noted Acts, namely:

Act of Indamnity: ordering all Catholics to be damned.

Act of Oblivion: ordering all Catholics to be oblivious, i.e., not to notice that they were damned.

Corporation Act: against fat Catholics, no Catholic being permitted to be more than five stone, dead weight.

Act of Uniformity: ordering all Catholics to look alike, but unlike Catholics, e.g., like Protestants, agreeing with the Deformation (see Hayden and Moonan).

Hoboes Corpses Act: ordering all Catholics, i.e., Hoboes, who still had bodies open or in hiding, to deliver them for the King's pleasure, to be made into corpses.

Five-Mile Act: ordering no Catholic to go within five miles of any person, place or thing, thus not being able to get a drink on a Sunday.

Thus religion went ahead greatly, due to a farmer named Tightus Oats inventing plots in which were piously executed many pious Catholics to discourage Bigotry, the Government being against it.

MIXED

Charles now climbing up an Oak Tree while the soldiers were looking on the ground, passed the Test Act to test the soldiers, they politely not noticing. His fruitful reign soon coming to an end, he passed an Act of Contrition, also saying as he passed out, 'Give poor Nell something to eat' (see Gwynn).

His reign was also noted for many other things, namely *The Great Plague of London,* not really great, not finishing the job; *The Great Fire of London,* not really great, not finishing the job, many things in London, however, being both plague-proof and fire-proof.

Charles' reign was also responsible for the Restoration, namely to build an Established Church in Ireland, also to give tights to the clergy to keep them respectable, the Irish not wanting to give them. In this reign also occurred Newton (Bramley Seedling), the discoverer of Gravy, Milton (false

Tights for Clergy

teeth), Locke (whiskey), Dryden (dry den), the Binominal Theorem (exam. papers), the Observer at Greenwich (pronounced Grin Itch) and many other things, these things being known as Miscellaneous, being different, not Battles (see Lecky).

SHOP-KEEPERS

Cromwell not being dead enough, was now dug up to die poperly for the King's pleasure, being hanged round the neck at Tieburn. Cromwell now said piously, with the Bible in both hands, 'Do unto others as they would do to you,' whereupon his wart was salted in a box to be hung up in all the towns of the Kingdom. After which the wart was taken to Hampton Court, where in life it loved so little, in death it is loved too well, being now very small from chips being sold off it to foreign tourists, the English being a nation of Shopkeepers, also chips stolen by vandolls who don't care (see Police).

FOOLISH

James the Twice (surnamed Just Stuart) was a brother of Charles the Twice, which was foolish. He was also a son of his father, thus loved by the Irish as his father was, which was foolish both times, for the Irish. He was also a Catholic which was foolish, going up on the throne to rule people wishing to change their wives for new ones, this now being the custom also with motor cars, the used one, however, being taken in part payment, unlike used wives, some used ones, however, being quite good and fresh in appearance if washed, nevertheless being good value to people not too particular, these being motor cars, not wives (see Bluebeard).

BABY

James now gave birth to a son, which was foolish at his age, the English being against children, as is the custom. So the people said to James without affection. Take away that empty

With Baby

baby,' and sent for William, surnamed Orange (from being yellow with thick skin), to come over and be their King without tissue, also being Protestant. William came, upon which all the people hailed him, saying aloud: 'Pip, pip hooray!' James fled to France (with baby) and then came back to Ireland, with Frenchmen, to win back his crown, being ready to fight bravely to the last drop of blood of the last Irishman, including Sarsfield, from saying aloud about his blood leaking, 'Oh that this were leaking for Ireland,' Irishmen being careless about their blood (see Doctor). William was also ready to fight, being a blood Orange.

JACKABITE

Thus was begun the Jackabite War, also called the Willabite War, also the War of the Resolution from James trying to make up his mind. It was a very romantic war, giving rise to Patrick Sarsfield of Lucan (ice-cream) also jackets (green), cockades (green and white), mess-tents (full), glasses (set), veterans (full), Blacksmiths (Limerick), Brigades (fire), Rapparees (Raps), Hogan (galloping), also Eamonn a Crick and Sean O Duibhir Alanna (see Ballad).

Eamonn a Crick

DARRY

The first battle was fought at Derry (pronounced Darry) with walls and gates shut by Walkers, this not being really a battle but a squeege, the Oranges being besqueeged from without, also from the Irish bump across the river. Horsflesh now went to ten shillings per lb., dogs' heads to fifteen shillings each, tallow twenty-four shillings a pound, and a certain fat man seeing the hungry soldiers looking at him, hid himself, saying without affection, 'No surrandhar, no provandhar,' thus keeping the cost of living up.

The Irish bump now however being bumped by three ships, the Orangemen and Orangewomen, also applewomen were relieved. Thus Darry was held solidly for the foreigner as is still the custom, due to Sir Jerry Mander, M.P. (see Basil-brooke).

ALL WET

The next fight in the Willabite fight was the Battle of the Boyne, peradventure being scarcely a battle, James losing his crown in the river and stopping to look for it. William coming up with a deep thrust in James' rear, it being, alas! unprotected, overthrew him into the water, thus causing James to say with asperity, 'Change things with me or I'll fight you again.' William did fight again with shrewd thrusts upon which James, getting cold feet from Boyne water, ran off to warm them. Meeting Lady Tirconnell in Dublin, he said with royal dignity, 'My Majesty have won the race,' and went off to France to win other races (see Righ Shamus he has gone, etc.).

ODDS

Thus William to his surprise won the Battle of the Boyne (see Macaulay), from James having held it in the wrong place and getting cold feet, also from William having forty thousand soldiers against twenty-six, an old English custom. This, however, did not take from his great victory, his attack and defence being very good, though not equal to James's footwork in the loose. The Irish did not play the game, not being good at foreign games as is now the custom, thus causing James to lose the Triple Crown.

Thus was lost the Battle of the Boyne, which was very historic, now also affectionately known to all the people as the Twalfth, Dolly's Bray, and To Hall with the Pope, the Orangemen and the Orangewomen, also applewomen, being pious, as well as against Bigotry. It was, however, a good battle for the student of history, being held on a date easy to remember, viz., 1960 (see Calendar).

CROOSTING

William now wanted to take Limerick, also noted for hams, lace and women. Sarsfield having no Honour galloped off in the dark with Galloper Hogan to meet the train from Waterford, it being full of William's guns. The train was stopped at Ballyneety owing to bad coal, an old English custom, the soldiers meanwhile playing pontoon in their boots.

Sarsfield came out from Ardnacrusha in the dark, the E.S.B. being short of water, (as was the custom), and the sentry, putting his gun up to his eye called sharply 'Halt, are you the password?' whereupon Sarsfield being noted for ready wit replied, 'I am,' and dashed past. The English soldiers now died suddenly, not of broken hearts, as Sarsfield and his men blew up the guns. William now being furious made a hole in the walls of Limerick with secondhand guns, and peeped in. De Lauzun the French officer said for a joke to paste him

Belles of St. Mary's

with Rosen apples. De Rosen the French officer said for a joke to paste him with Lauzun apples, also to blow up the Black Market. The women of Limerick, however, being no joke, croosted him out with paving stones and bottles, saying aloud (without affection), 'Who wants the big rotten Orange?' thus striking terror into the heart of William and his men, an old custom with Limerick women, still in a good state of preservation, to strike terror into the hearts of men.

RIVER TO CROSS

Athlone was a good battle being fought well in the Irish Custume, eleven Irishmen breaking down the bridge which the English wanted to cross, the eleven Irish men being bravely attacked by the whole English army with shot and shell. These eleven having lost their lives by cannon balls in this fierce and bloody battle, eleven other Irish came out to knock the planks, being unreasonable, knowing the English had one more river to cross. Again the English fired off their big guns with great military skill and daring. Two cowardly Irishmen remained, dodging between the cannon balls as they passed. Being still unreasonable they pulled down the planks, and being afraid to fight the English, they swam home. Whereupon St. Root, saying, 'I have seen no deed like that in France' (see de Vere), became careless, letting the English steal in the back door, thus losing Athlone.

HEAD LOST

St. Root the French officer also lost the battle of Aughrim through taking off his hat to say 'The day is ours, boys' (see Joyce). A cannon ball coming that way hit his head which was unprotected, thus he was completely killed, his lifeless body falling afterwards to the ground. This was sad because if his head had been in his hat at the time, the cannon ball would

Would have passed

have passed by. St. Root now telling nobody to take his place, being jealous of Sarsfield, the battle of Aughrim was lost. Hats are useful to keep heads in.

TREATY

William now being gone back to England to invent the National Debt, the English won the second siege of Limerick by means of Treaty (broken), an old English custom. The Treaty was soon made upon a stone (now mounted on a pedestrian in Limerick for tourists to see). The purple ink, however, did not dry, this being the time of no blotting paper, whereupon the English broke it. Limerick is, therefore, now known to tourists as the City of the Violet Treaty, also noted for Treaty bars, Treaty sausages, and Garryowen in Glory Tobacco, being very historic. Glotting paper is useful.

LATE

The French army now arrived up the Shannon to help the Irish, being late, as was the custom, being too long on the say (see Shan Van Vocht). So Sarsfield and his men now having nothing else to do, rode down the glen, also going on the say, thus giving rise to Sarsfield's men being known as Splashers brave and true.

They all went off to France to win every nation's battles but their own (see Ballad), thus giving rise on far foreign fields to

Wild

geese (wild), Brigades (Irish), Co. Clare (Dragoons), Fontenoy (huts), Ramillies (bloody fields), Ypres (choir), etc., this all being very romantic but sad R.I.P. they all having fell and passed away but good men like you men are plenty here today (see Fairy Tales).

PENAL CODE

Ireland was now still full of Catholics who being unreasonable would not go and die out to give room to the Protestants who not being many, were nevertheless very important from having the new religion, also being the Assendancy.

So the English not wanting to kill off Catholics by use of bloody arms (the English often getting hurt doing this, being also soft-hearted) now tried peaceful means, inventing the Penal Laws, so called from being the most penal in the world, this making the English noted. These also were called the Penal Cowed by English with nice accents, wishing to cow the Irish. The Penal Cowed was as follows:—

Religion: All Catholic clergy excepting circular clergy should leave Ireland for ever, also stay away, those not doing so being adjudged guilty of Height Reason, and hanged, drawn and slaughtered Priests' heads were five pounds each Registered priests (postage extra) were told to die out and let nobody take their places. Nobody could ring a bell or a steeple. Priests were shot at sight or later. Protestants could take Catholic churches and keep them. They did.

Education: Teachers' heads were £1 each, bald heads 2/6 extra, looking better salted in a box, thus the Cost of Living went up. No teacher could teach children anything in public, private, or elsewhere, even in hedges. No children could learn anything anywhere, the English wanting to make the Irish more ignorant than the English themselves. This was impossible.

No school could have a playground, a washbasin, a good lavatory, a good fire in winter, good walls or roof or furniture or pictures, this being to give rise to the dirty Irish.

Some traces of the Penal Cowed still remain.

Bald Extra

Property: No Catholic could keep his own arms or put his hands in his pockets, or have a horse which could carry more than five pounds. When a Catholic died he could not keep his own land, it being gravelled among his sons to make them poor, this being Gravelkind from olden times but different.

General: No Catholic could have anything, do anything, get anything, give anything, take anything, keep anything, be anything, say anything, go anywhere, come anywhere, stay anywhere, live anywhere or die anywhere, except out.

But the Catholics being unreasonable, albeit being made Poor, Miserable, Wretched, Oppressed, Depressed, Degraded, and Beggared in their own country would not die out, thus making England sad (see Savory).

GORGE THE FIRST

Gorge the First of the Sixth had a good appetite, also a glorious rein following Queen Anne, now, however, known as the Dead Queen. He also had a vote, being Elector of Hangover, thus founding the House of Brunswick Black, or the Hangover Period. He was, therefore, a great English King through being a German with no English, also through not being mostly insane like Gorge the Third, who had not yet occurred. At his court, however, morality was, unhappily, very laxative.

RIOT ACT

In this rein was passed the Riot Act to keep twelve people from having a row for an hour at a time. This was done by reading the Act to them aloud, whereupon they stopped fighting and went off to another public house. This was known

Reading Riot Act

as Riot and Civil Commotion, the English being always Riot, also very Civil even when fighting.

Gorge the First also told the Old Pretender to stop pretending and go off to France, where tourists can pretend all they like, being far from home.

GOOD LAWS

The members of the Irish Parliament got positions, titles, bribes, and middle-age pensions from the English, the English being very nice. This made the Parliament like England and pass everything which the English wanted. This Parliament was also fond of Ireland when not taken up with being fond of England. So, seeing the Irish people working too hard, they passed laws to stop Irish trade, to make the tired Irish people rest themselves. This made the Irish people start complaining again, the Irish people already being called the cry-babies of the western world from complaining out loud when murdered or robbed by the English. Taxes being put on the goods the Irish people now took to snuggling around the coast in seaside places, an old custom still in a good state of preservation, the people also now snuggling across the border. The Government tried to stop snuggling by means of gaugers going around searching every-

Snuggling across the Border

where. Snuggling will stop, however, when the country is all joined together and no border and the people united. The natural resources of the country will be developed and the balance of payments will be good.

BONY PRINCE

Gorge's rein was also noted for the Young Pretender or Cock of the North, thus giving rise to the old saying 'What the old cock crows the young cock knows.' Going on a Highland Fling be defeated the English at Potsan Pans. This was through the treachery of Lock Heel, head of the Cameroons, not warning the English that a Cameroon never must yield, also to the treachery of other Heels, upon which the Young Pretender, getting thin from sleeping out in a kilt in the heather glen, now became known as Bony Prince Charlie. Thus with thirty thousand pounds on his head and nothing in his pocket he was thrown overboard on the blasted heath by Bloody Cumberland and he began to use bad language. But he got up again, and had many vissitissitudes until he was helped to escape by Ramsay MacDonald pretending to be a girl. He went off to France, saying that he would be new coming back again, and there he stopped pretending and got drunk.

The Irish loved Bony Prince Charlie through being let down by his grandfather, his great-grandfather and all belonging to him; this being a romantic old Stuart tradition.

The Old Pretender was the father of the Young Pretender, all because of his pretending. He died in frightful poverty.

GORGE III. 1760—1820

Gorge III was divided into three parts (see Oxford History) from having too long a rein and this made him mad. He was noted for sacred societies, namely Whiteboys going around Munster in the night with their shirts hanging out, these being white at that time, knocking ditches and throwing landlords into dikes full of briars. This was to stop the landlords putting ditches round the commoners which were always grazed by all the people. Father Sheehy was tried for unrolling Whiteboys, also for murdering a man who went to America to pretend to be dead. Father Sheehy was innocent in Dublin but guilty in Clonmel where it was easy to be guilty, being the chief town of the Ascendancy in County Tipperary, now, however, noted for being the seat of the County Council, and other canned meat, also cider, girls' shoes, and greyhounds. Fr. Sheehy was executed by the English, and the man he murdered came home.

The Protestants also had a sacred society called Heads of Oak from being like old oak trees. They were going around in the night time attacking the big people, also Heads of Steel attacking men in the middle for going between the landlords and the tenants.

TEA PARTY

The American war was caused by England wanting to rain over America, also by England giving a mad tea-party in a ship called the Mayfly, and wanting the Americans to pay for it, England always wanting America to pay for everything. This was aggravated by the revolting Americans throwing their tea leaves over their shoulders into the water, they having no manners and no slop bowels. This is now known in history as The Bostoon's Tea-Party. It caused the War of Impudence, the Americans being full of it.

GREAT DAY

The English getting offended from having nice manners, said they would make the Americans pay through the nose for that, this also being due to the dollar position being bad; but the Americans answering back through the nose, said they would not pay. The English then tried to kill all the people, but this rose up George Washingtub who could not tell a lie when his father caught him cutting down his lettle cherry tree with his little acts. George Washingtub hunted the English and made a Declaration of Impudence in a draught it also being signed by

His little acts

an Irishman named Mr. Carroll, Irish Pressebetiarians from Ulster being the cause of it all.

This said that nobody should try to put nothing over on nobody without telling him why, and one man is as good as another and maybe a lot better. So the English had to go home on 4th July, on a Tuesday, and it is still a great day in America.

GRATTAN'S PARLIAMENT

Mr. Grattan's Parliament was now free but it was full of rotten seats, one noble lord having sixteen seats which was too much for one man, and which he sold at elections, which was a rotten thing to do. One man in Belturbet got eleven thousand pounds, not of our money, for his rotten seat. The Catholics being only four-fifths of the population could not sit in Parliment from having no seats, and no money to pay for rotten ones, not having yet got Catholic Amansapation. The Parliment was full of politicans. It also contained some educated men who also worked for their living, as is the custom.

THE GULLETINE

The French Revolution was also thought of by Charles Dickens in a great book called The Scarlet Pimp or Nell. This made the Protelariat also called the Sands Cullotys, rise up and shout out loud for three things, namely Libertie, Legalitie, Eternitie. The well-off people got a drive around the town in big cars called tundras while the poorer women were darning socks. They were took to the big gulletine and there they were all gulleted, crying out: 'It is a far far better thing to do than to be ever done.' They were called raristocrats and their '*bl—y heads fell into *bl—y baskets, and the people all shouted out "Vivvy la Republicue!"' This was an awful *bl—dy Revelootion, from everyone being gulleted, and bleeding like anything.

DRUNK

A big jail in Paris named the Bastible fell down one day, and all the prisoners ran out. The King was blamed for this and he was gulleted. His name was Lousi XVI. The Queen, Marie Antoniowette, who was a nice girl, was also gulleted for telling the people to eat sweet cake. The people did not want sweet cake, but they all broke into a public house after hours and got drunk from drinking port wine out of a busted barrel. (See Dickens.)

WOLF TONE

Wolf Tone was the dog of Ireland with the harp and the shamrock, also the greatest Irishman that ever lived. He was also a great man from being the father of all the Irish Republicans. He was born in Dublin one night in 1763. His people came from Kildare, but it was before that. He was not a Catholic nor a Prodestan, but an acrostic meaning no God, but all the same he was healthy. He was young and clever and good. He finished

* bloody

84

his schooling in Trinity College, the stronghole of the Assendancy, and he got good at arguing. Being a nice man he treated the Catholics very well and he did not like to talk about them. He began a Catholic Sociation in Belfast with Somairle MacNeill, and they said that everyone should get their rights. After a while himself and Napper Tandy put up another Sociation in Dublin. They put branches of it here and there by degrease, but it was all Prodestans until the year 1794. Then it was made into a sacred society to let in the Catholics.

GREAT ACT

The Catholics got a great Act in 1793 from the Irish Parliment. The two-pound Catholics, also known as Forty shillings, could now vote, but with their left hand only. The Catholics could now also go into Trinity College to get degrease. Trinity College is still in a good state of preservation, and all Catholics can now go in there, to look at the Book of Kells. They could also be juries and carry their arms with them.

Two-pound Catholic

PHYSIC FORCE

The United Irishmen, though mostly Prodestans, now said they would use Physic Force also well known as fight, like the Tears Etat in France, and they started negotiations with the people in France. Mr. Tone went to France to see Mr. Roche about some ships, and some men, and Mr. Roche said he would come. So Mr. Roche got seventeen warships and thirteen friggets full of men and they sailed off out of Breast to Ireland.

BAD WEATHER

But there was a big stone in the sea and one of the ships hit up again it, and it got broke and spilled out twelve hundred of the men and they all got drownded. Four other ships sailed up again one another because the day was foggy. More ships went astray in fowl winds from not knowing the way, or maybe from tretchery, which nobody knows. More of them came to Bantry Bay and the fishermen girls came swinging baskets at them to welcome them. But the weather got bad, as was the custom, and this made the French General grouchy. So they cut the ropes that were tying the ships and the French people went home, not liking bad weather.

The French are always famous for helping us only for being late, or bad weather. The weather was always against Ireland.

SPIES

The Britches Government heard about the plans of the United Irishmen by means of having spies to tell them, all Governments except ours now having spies in other countries to steal around in the dark and spy on other nations and find out their business. This is now known as espyonage so as not to sound mean like spying, so that Governments can still pretend to be honourable. (Not our Governments.)

'98

The Great Rebellion of '98 is now very famous from having been held in '98 which is now a very famous year from having a great Rebellion held in it namely, Who Fears to Speak of '98. The English getting vexed from being afraid of France, wanted to fight somebody without an army, also they wanted to blame the Irish Parliament for not being able to keep the people quiet. This would be a good excuse for England to ebolish the Irish Parliament and join England to Ireland, the English being good at Unions with other countries to save all the people from themselves. This is known as Conquest. It is a noble thing when done by England, but not when done by other countries like Germany, these being fond of Aggression, which England bravely fights against.

CAUSE OF

The people of Wexford being unreasonable were the main cause of the Rising, through not liking the North Cork Milesians, the

Heshons, the Yo-Yo's and other soldiers to be going around maiming, torturing, killing, robbing, looting and burning all the

Heart and Hand and Scythes

people, this being their duty, which England expected them to do like their dessendants the Black and Tans. The people of Wexford told them to stop, also the nice Protestants in the north, namely Henry Joy McCracker, being unbiggeted. The people having no guns or ammunician fought with heart and hand. They also fought with scythes. How they did this nobody knows. The people all backed them up and they got free lodgings in all the houses. This was known as Rackrent, from the Rackrents now living in the house of Kelly the Boy at a place called Killann. The Rackrents are great hurlers.

FAIR TRIAL

Admirable Bumper then came from France in a ship with Wolf Tone. Admirable Bumper attacked the British Navy with his ship, and there was a great fight for six months, which the British Navy bravely won with rulers for measuring the wave. Tone fought bravely but he was captured and sent in an iron lung to Dublin, iron lungs now also being used to keep porter in.

The English having arranged to hang him, gave him a very fair trial (see Casement). Wolf Tone said to shoot me shoot me like a soldier and not like a dog, being the dog of Ireland, but they said it was all a matter to him and he would have to be satisfied with being hung.

They were going to hang him in the morning to make him feel ashamed of himself, the English being fond of hanging men and women. But so as to have they not have the satisfaction of it, he trottled himself the night before his death, and when the man came into his cell in the morning he was too dead to hang him. This was after the English cut his trote, saying he trottled himself, which he never done.

UNION

Mr. Pit, the British Prime Minister, now wanted to join England to Ireland for the good of the country, also for the good of England. He made Lord Cornwarts Lord Leftenant of Ireland, and Cuttrote Castlereagh Chief Secetry to help him to pass the Union. All the Protestants got millions of Irish money for their rotten seats (not of our money). They also got grand gobs and brides and titles and pensions to make them go into the Union, now also known as the Workhouse. They also told everyone they would give Catholic Amansapation which they did not give. Anyone who said the Union should not be invented was sacked out of his job, also his cousins with him. The people looked on the Union with abborrents but it was done all the same. Then Lord Castlereagh cut his own trote with a razor which must have been very sharp, for no penknife would cut his trote. He was not a genial and kindly personality and he was not held in great esteem in the locality, not being a strong supporter of the Nationalist cause. His death did not cast a gloom and the cortege which followed his remains to his last resting place was not of unusually large dimensions. There is a grand poem about the Union telling everybody that Lord Castlereagh was a tool of Satin which means the Devil in poetry. His epithet was wrote by Lord Byron, namely 'Posterity will nare survey a nobler grave than this,' etc. Castlereagh was the father of corruption.

UNITED

Ireland was now joined on to England in spite of her. Ireland and England were now one country namely the United Kingdom, this being known as the freedom of small nations like Little Belgium. Ireland now got a lot of liberty from England, the English being noted for ruling well in India and South Africa and other places which they were minding for all the people. Ireland was now free to keep her own national debt and also to pay some of England's. Irish people could now go over and be Members of Parliament in England, except the Catholics. These were only a vass majority and they could not go until they would swear on oath that the Catholic Religion was the okium of the people (see Stalin). They would not do this, being unreasonable, and so the English tried to please them by giving them numerous fine promises. This did not increase production, also Ireland got poor from England taking all her money and forgetting to give it back. This did not increase production and the balance of payments got worse for Ireland, as Dr. Johnson said it would, telling us not to unite with them or they would rob us. That was why Stella died of a broken heart, in frightful poverty.

ROBBIT EMMET

Robbit Emmet is now well-known as the greatest Irishman that ever lived, also as the darlin of Eiryin, having told no one to daar to write his epithet. He was the younger son of his father and he was born one night in the year seventh hundred and seventy eight. Then he made up his mind to start an army and he began to gather every man that was around the streets of Dublin.

Robbit had a very high mind, also some very high spirits. At the age of fifteen he was a growing-up boy and his father told him to go to Trinity College now noted for the Book of Kells which should not be there. Robbit formed a Close scholarship also, taking up with the French Revelution and he got very dramatic and earnest. Trinity College did not like him, not liking French Revelutins which were not nice like English ones so he left Trinity College so as to have they not have the satisfaction of hunting him out of it.

HONEST

Robbit Emmet now often went listening to old Moor's poems and he often gave them to his schoolmeats to read, Old Moor being also known as Othello in a play by Shakepeare who was, however, only an Englishman.

Robbit Emmet was very honest and he said he would kill all the English if they did not go home to their own country and leave Ireland to the people that ownded it. This was known well in later Irish history as 'Break the Collection' namely to stop England collecting all our money and taking it home.

ROW

But the English would not go home so Robbit spent all his pocket money making spikes and other guns to hunt the English, having an Arsenall in Dublin. Then he went out into the streets and all the corner boys came to help him, nobody but corner boys ever wanting to fight against England to hunt them out of places that did not belong to them. Then every thing went wrong and his Arsenall blew up.

The corner boys did not fight, only kicked up a row in the streets, killing a kind and human Englishman, so Emmet had to go away. The English heard about him from a retch of a spy named McNally, he not having a nice name like espyonadge agent. The English called to Emmet's house but the girl said he was out.

HANGING

They said to the girl that they would give her 5,000 lbs. to tell them where the boss was gone but the girl said she would not. Her name was Annie Devlin and she is one of the bravest women in Irish history from not telling, which is very brave for a woman. Then the English soldiers forgetting that English people are always shivalry, namely kind to girls, said they would hang Annie if she would not tell. So they tied her on to the shaft of the horses' car and and heeled up the car to hang her. They half hung her but she would not tell, so they did not hang her dead because of shivalry, also because she could not tell them, if hung. They only prodded her with bayonets then. She died a lot later on, in frightful poverty.

Half-hung

FAIR TRIAL

Robbit Emmet had a girl named Sarah Currant who was his finance and he was mad about her and she was mad about him. He could go away only he stayed behind to see her and he was caught in the act. He got a very fair trial (see William Joyce) from a great English Judge named Norbury, his mottow being Hang'em First, British Justice being well-known even in these ancient times. When Sarah heard that her boy friend was to be hung the poor girl nearly went mad.

GREAT

Daniel O'Connell was the greatest Irishman that ever lived, his heart to Rome, his soul to God, his body to Ireland, and other things to Caherciveen (see Folklore). This was from being born in Kerry, now also noted for footballers and mountains.

Daniel had the Kerry accent, also a polite accent for talking to big people, and so he was too smart for all the big English liars in court. His mottow was 'Ciall agus Neart' meaning 'Have sense for yourself and get strong.'

Daniel was a big fat man and he was called 'The Liverater.' He was good to look at, driving in a coach and four through Parliment with boots that cost fourpence (not of our money), things being cheap then. He never spoke Irish because he was too good-looking, also because he belonged to the well-off people, Irish being only for poor people, as is now the custom, poor people now being very scarce however, owing to Sociable Welfare Bills, and other bills, not paid.

EDUACATION

Daniel went off to France to get Eduacation, France being always a great place to get eduacated in, also the Irish Catholics being let have no schools at home owing to their knowing too much already for the English.

Daniel got well eduacated in France. He also saw a lot of blood in the Fench Revelution and he did not like it, so when he came home he said he would not spill bloodshed, only fight for the Catholics with his tongue. He fought one man, however, who dared him, with a pistil and a glove. This was a jewel and he had to kill him but he got sorry. He also had a row with Biddy Morarty out of his jommertry and he put her down by saying to her not to be a miserable submultitude of a dewplacate racyo of a one-sided parlellagraph. The English wanted to poison him one night by putting pepper in his glass. But the servant girl in England was an Irish girl, as is the custom, and she sang an Irish song and knocked the candle to make Daniel O'Connell stop drinking the poison, and he stopped.

GRINDING

Daniel got to be a great solicitor up in Dublin and he fought hard for all the people with his talk, also by holding monstrous meetings every place but in Clontawf, formerly noted for nice people and a fierce battle, and now noted for nothing. This was to stop the English grinding down the Catholics, not letting them get jobs or go into Parliment, the Catholics being nothing in their own land but a vass majority which was no good (see Stalin). Daniel was also known as the Councillor from being great at arguing and saving people who were summonsed by the English, mostly for nothing. In his spare time he used to write things in the paper to beat the English, which he did. Papers are powerful from being able to put in anything they like to make all the people believe it, and they all do, including lies.

PROFIT

Daniel was great for getting all the people to wake up and follow him because he was the father of Consequentional Agitation. The people had sunk into inershee and he stirred them up and welded them. This made them strong to fight, but the Government made a law to put down all the people. Daniel put them all up again with another name, by driving a horse and car through the Government. So he got all the Catholics to come together and every man that would have a penny to give it to the man at the door with the box. Then he went around and gathered up the votes of the people.

There was a vacuum in the County Clare and all the people said it would do grand for Daniel O'Connell's seat, to make a show of the English. There was a great election, a man by the name of Fitzgerald, with a good father one time, going against Daniel to please the English. The journey of Daniel from Limerick to Ennis was like the walk of a king with everybody shouting, and thirty hundred thousand people slept out all night in Ennis in the rain without a drink, to hear Daniel. When the pole was counted Daniel had two votes to every one for the man of England. All the people of Dublin followed him down to Kerry in their carriages and the people of Kerry burned all the furze bushes making bonefires. So he won the election, as he said he would, Daniel being a prophet.

ASHAMED

Then Daniel went over to England and the English gave him the book to take the vote against the Catholic religion to say it was the okium of the people, but he would not do it. He said 'Ye can throw me out but I won't go out for ye.' Then the whole world heard about it and the English nearly got ashamed, except the King, who was not a very respectable man. They said they would give Catholic Emancipatience and so Daniel relieved all the people and they were all mad about him. The two-pound Catholics however were not freed. Daniel was the best man in the world to give a speech and he could be heard everywhere.

TIGHTS

The Tight War took place about this time long ago. The English wanted to give tights to the Prodestan clergy to keep them in comfort. The tights were a tent of all the people had. They were not the same all over the country, some being heavy and some light. The people did not want to give the tights to the tight clergy, from not wanting Prodestan clergy for nothing at all. The tight clergy often had to do without anything and they were in great distress from being already very imperishable. The Government said they would make the people do it and they used to send the Tight Procktors all around the country to take the tights off all the people. There was a Tight battle at Carrickshock and it shocked all the people, several pheasants being killed and also eleven policemen. Fifty people also got killed in the County Cork trying to stop the Government from taking the tights off a widow. Then the Government got ashamed and they ordained that the Prodestan clergy would have to get their tights from the landlord.

SCHOOLS

The English Government would not let the Catholics have Schools or Eduacation. This was to abolish the Irish mind and character and make all the Catholics illegiterate. The Catholic children did not like this, being mad for eduacation, as is now the custom, and wanting to go to school because they would not be let. So the people invented Hedge Schools, namely sitting on furze bushes inside the ditch with sacred schoolmasters talking Latin and Matamics with one small head to carry all the news. The English called this 'feloniously to learn,' but it was really Hedge Schools, and they were all good scholars from the good masters, but no mistresses. The girls had to go somewhere else. Goldsmith said the furze bushes were 'unprofitable gay,' and the master a man severe he was, which he had to be.

NATIONAL

About this time, after a long time, namely 1831, the English said they would have schools and eduacation for the Catholics. This was to make them like England, eduacation being great for this purpose, only the ignorant Irish not liking England, also the ignorant Indians, also some ignorant Americans nowadays, not wanting to pay for everything for England. There are ignorant people in Africa also, called Ma Ma.

All the scholars in the new schools in Ireland should learn out of a book that 'the country we live in was not always called England.' They should also sing 'I am a happy English child' and grow up into happy English men and also women, and so the new schools were called National Schools. The master in every school should put a big card up on the wall telling him to 'act in a spirit of obedience to the law and loyalty to his Sovran,' and not to be telling the little children what the English did.

PROGRAMME

All the scholars were to learn to read, write, and siphon, this being the nice English name for sums. There was not to be any Irish in the schools, this being only the language of the Catholics, who were only a vass majority which is no good (see Stalin). Every scholar was to have a big pole tied out of his neck, and a big cut put in it with a hatchet every time he said a word of Irish, and if he had a lot of cuts he would be flogged to death with the pole in the evening, or maybe with the hatchet. This was to help him to forget Irish and learn English, and it was sometimes the cause of bad attendance, like minding the child.

BUILDINGS

The schools were built all over the country, mostly in places where nothing else could be built. They had no immunities outside for the children, only boreens and fields, but nevertheless they got on well being still there in great numbers. The number of illegiterates went down, but they did not make the scholars into a happy English child. All the scholars in them now learn to talk Irish, the language of our great ancestors of long ago, also the language, unhappily, of our bad ancestors of long ago.

All the people now want Irish, from it being the tongue of the Gael. Nobody talks it yet, but all the people are learning it hard for thirty years, and they are going to speak it very soon, and then Ireland will be not nearly free nearly but also Gaelic nearly as well.

OLD

Daniel O'Connell said about this time that he would win Repeal off the English, namely to get them to put the Union down. He went to big meetings all over the country and all the people came to cheer him. The English would not let him have a meeting in Clontawf. They stopped the meeting with 4,000 soldiers, big guns, and warships, namely fearful odds, and they put Daniel in jail to stop him telling everybody in the world what they were doing to Ireland. The House of Lords said to let him out again, some few English Lords being strangely in favour of fair play. Then he went through the streets of Dublin up on top of a big high car, and all the people burned all the bushes making bonfires for him.

Daniel then got old, and he said he would go to Rome to see the Pope to have his heart cut out, maybe to show that it was not broken. So he started off but he got sick in Genoa, now noted for Christopher Colombus, who found out America, which nobody guessed was there, except the Americans, being good at guessing. Lots of people found out America afterwards. Daniel died in Genoa in frightful poverty and they cut out his heart with a big knife after he was dead, as he said to do, and they posted it on to the Pope in a glass case. They brought the rest of him back to Ireland and barried it under a big Round Tower in a place called Glasnevin Symetry, now noted for tombstones. Daniel's ruins can be seen to this day in Carhan in the County Kerry, also the O'Connell Memorial Church in Caherciveen. This is so called from Daniel O'Connell's burst being up in the window in the porch, made of marbles. There is also a great picture of Daniel in the National Gallery with his hand where his heart was. Lots of people are called after him from being a great man and showing all the people how to stand up for themselfs in Ireland and Europe. He did not speak compulsory Irish and some people did not like that, some great men, however, not speaking compulsory Irish down to recent times, including now. Daniel got a big statue up in Dublin, with girls all round him, now with bullet holes, from the Rising, not listening to him at all. Nelson got a bigger statue and he have it yet, in the middle of Dublin.

NOT JOLLY

William the Fourth was exceeded by his niece Victoria, who was called after a London railway station often in detective stories. She could not, however, exceed him in Hangover, because of the Salient Law. This made her serious.

Queen Victoria was the only child of a widow of an old and respected family. The widow trained her very well for the lofty position she was to fill (see Oxfoot History). She filled it very well, from being fat, but she was not jolly. She was, however, very respectable, and she would not go around in shorts like hikers. She did not know who to marry, but in the end it was the Prince of Sacks Coal Bug got her. He was called the Prince Concert from being always singing and getting up concerts. He was not, however, as respectable as the Queen and so he always had to walk behind her, and he died suddenly in 1861.

The Queen was very big in herself, being still noted for biggetry and she would not let anybody sit down or laugh while she was looking. Loose Carroll wrote a lot of books to amuse her, namely Alice Where art thou and other books on Matamatics. She said Alice was good but she would not please him to laugh. I saw her once in the pictures. Pictures are great for eduacation, being now used in many good schools.

HUNGRY

Ireland at the time was noted for many fine famines, the Irish getting hungry to make a show of the English, also dying, to make the English ashamed, if possible. There was a famine in Connacht in 1831, but it was not very historical from not being big enough. The British Empire was noted for many fine famines.

BLACK

There was a very good famine in Ireland in '47. The Irish people got hungry in '45, but the English did not get ashamed. They got hungry again in '46, and also in '47. This was due to sixteen million of Sir Walter Raleigh's bad potatoes getting black, so it was called Black '47. The people then had nothing to eat, only cattle and wheat and corn. The English took these away, to England, and told all the people to eat the black potatoes. The people, being unreasonable would not do this, only went eating nettles and other quare things. Then they began to die of hunger and the English said the famine was a great success. Then the people began to die in heaps everywhere around the place, millions of them. Their imasiated bodies were took away in big horse loads and berried all together in big pits like dead dogs with no coffins.

SHAME

When they were nearly all dead the deacent English people began to get ashamed. The Government did not, however, get ashamed yet. The English people made up some money, and they also sent some bags of flour to Ireland. The Sultan of Turkey heard about the terrible starvation in Ireland, and he said he would give twenty thousand pounds to the collection. Queen Victoria was very sad at the starving Irish, and she sent a very nice letter saying her heart bled for her Irish people dying in millions in the ditches and she sent over five pounds to feed them all. Then the English said the Sultan should take back his twenty thousand pounds and not have it to have people have it to say that he was as good as the Queen. But the Sultan gave five hundred pounds in spite of the English, who said the Sultan insulted the Queen.

EXILES

Then the starving Irish people said they would go off to America to get bread and work for all, also sunshine. So they stopped sitting on the style and they went off into coffin ships and they all got thrown into the ocean where they died in frightful poverty when the coffin ships sank from being rotten, also from being drove by sales instead of engines, and the weather stormy. Some of the ships were blew to America and the people got cured and then they made a great nation out of America from being the Exiles of Eryin also the inventors of Emigration. America is now full of their ancestors, having millions and millions of people with Irish blood in their muscles.

MEAL

When the people were nearly all dead or gone the English Government said they would relieve them. They got a lot of yellow meal for the people from India, the famine now being over in that country and the next great one not yet begun. Then the English Government said they would make roads to nowhere and big piers of gates in the sea to be washed away. This was to make the starving people work. But the people, being ungrateful, kept on dying, and the ones that did not die turned against the English. This was from eating the yellow meal, in stirabout, which made them cross. Yellow meal is good for pigs and hens to make them lay. It is now very dear, and we should grow our own food and increase production.

RESULTS

The famine had great results for the English. It killed off most of the Irish people, and made beggars of the rest. This was a great victory for the English. It also sent off millions of Irish people to America, and these do not like England. This is not a good victory for England, for only for them the English would now be able to beg more money from America. They would also be able to get America to fight their battles better for them, some of the Irish people in America telling the Americans not to fight for England, also telling the English to get out of our six counties, and go home and mind their own country, now in a bad way, being full of Austerity.

LAND

In those days there was a lot of land in Ireland, and the landlords had it, having got it from the English who confistcated it from the Irish people who ownded it. These landlords were the Assendancy, and they would not give all the people the three Fs.

The Ulster people had a great interest in the land and this was called the Ulster Tenant Rite. They had a great meeting in Dublin one day in 1850 with priests and Pressbetarians and tenants and landlords and everybody. This was to be fair about the land and it was called the Irish Tenant Liege, to get the three Fs.

ASHES

The Phoenix Club was invented in Skibberreen in 1856 with an eagle eye on Russia. The Phoenix club was invented out of ashes which rose up again with the wind. The chief man in it was O'Donovan Rossa who was the greatest Irishman that ever lived. He was well liked by Patrick Pearse who went to his funeral, telling everybody he was a Fenian dead—and the English were fools three times to leave him be.

James Stephens got wounded in '48 and he put life into the Phoenix movement, and they went out in the dark to beat England by drilling up and down in the moonlight. But somebody told the English about them and the English did not like it. Kerry was very famous for Moonlight.

ADVANCE

This was a time of great advance from Sir Robert Peal having repealed the laws against Corns and making those who had them walk up and pay their Income Tax, except the farmers, who need not pay any Income Tax any time. Queen Victoria had about nine children, but a lot of them died, and then she got very fat. But she stayed very respectable and she would not go around in slacks, nor smoke cigarettes nor drink cocktales while anybody was looking. She was very fond of Ireland from giving 5 lbs. to stop the famine.

There was a great war with Russia known as the Crimay, in a place called Sepastobol. It was a Russian winter and Florence Nightingale used to sing sweetly to the soldiers to make them like the snow up to their necks in their bad clothes. This was the cause of Communists. Patrick Sheehan then went and got

Singing in the snow

blind within the trenches from not listening to Florence, but the English did not care, he being only an Irishman evicted out of the Glen of Aherlow. They put him in jail for trying to beg his bread, which caused him to say, Remember poor Blind Sheehan. English soldiers often say Blind me and other things too, different from Blind Sheehan.

MIGHT

The Irish farmers were now getting on bad, as is the custom, from not getting the three Fs. The English had took all their land an gave it to their own soldiers, thus giving rise to land-lords. Cromwell was one of the chief causes of this by piously murdering all the people with the bible in one hand and a sore in the other and a big wart on his nose which made him very cross. Taking all the land from all the people was a glorious victory, also known as conquest. The Germans tried to do this to other countries, and it was known as aggression, namely world domination, and England, being full of Honour, went out to fight them with Irish and American soldiers. The Russians also do it and it is called Communism. Nobody fights the Russians, but the Pope, the Russians being very strong. The Pope wants the Seventh Commandment to be for everybody. Big nations do not like the Seventh Commandment, only for other people, but they pretend to like it when they like. They have a nicer commandment for themselves, namely Might is Right. This is called bullying in school. Big nations praise themselves when they take everything a small nation has. They always have good excuses for doing this. It is known also as empire building, namely by murdering ignorant people to save them from themselves and rule them right. Ignorant people do not want to be ruled right, always wanting to stay ignorant and dirty and keep their own countries. The British Empire was made up of people ignorant and dirty in Ireland and India, also the Bores in Africa, and the Kikyuyus and Ma Ma.

MIDDLEMAN

The farmers were now only tenants in their own lands and they had to pay rackrent. The landlords were all over in England getting drunk and they had Agents in Ireland to send them the rent. The Agents used to gather the rackrent from all the people and keep a lot of it for theirselfs. They waxed fat on the Irish farmer, like everyone does to this day, and so they were called middlemen from having big middles, and they would not give the farmers the three Fs.

If a middleman saw a farmer smoking a cigarette or going to a dance he would raise his rackrent. A farmer could not get a new suit or whitewash his house, or sweep his yard or get a prize bull, or his rackrent would be raised. No farmer could have a motor car or a wireless or a bathroom to wash his wife and children in, or the middleman would come in in the middle of it and lift his rackrent. No farmer could be clean or make more money because the middlemen would take it all.

PITIFUL

Then the farmer could not pay any more and the middleman would bring the bayliff with a crow bar and batter and ram. The farmer would be threw out on the road with his sick wife and baby and feeble old mother and his house knocked down

100

for the bullock. Then they would all have to die in the dyke in frightful poverty with nettles in it, or to go to the poorhouse to be torn asunder without the three Fs. This gave rise to some farmers grumbling, an old custom still in a good state of preservation. The landlord might be a nice man sometimes, but he did not know about this from being drunk in England. Some landlords used to stay in Ireland and the farmers used to go

Another landlord shot

inside the ditch to shoot them on the way home. This was to frighten them, but often a farmer used to miss them, from being too hungry to hold the gun steady. This was pitiful. It gave rise to the old saying, 'Another landlord shot'; when he wasn't.

SACRED VOTING

There was a Prodestan rector in Donegal, a nice man not biggetted, named Mr. Butt, which is also sometimes a conjunction or a bit of a cigarette too short to smoke anymore. Mr. Butt had a son who was the greatest Irishman that ever lived, for a while. His father called him Isaac with the bible in one hand but no sore in the other. When Isaac got big he said he would win Home Rule for all the people, also the three Fs. This was to have T.D.'s of our own to get jobs for all the people, namely by pull, which is useful, being better than education.

The Ballad Act was passed in 1872 to make all the people go to the pole and vote without nobody knowing about it in a boot, and put it into a box except they were illiterature. This was called the Ballad Box from all the songs the people put into it with their votes. It is also known as sacred voting. The land-lords did not like it, because they could not make the people vote for themselves any more. Then there was a General Election in 1874, and all the people went to the Ballad Boxes and put in 60 Home Rulers to fight peacefully and pass Home Rule without physic and force. But the English would not let them.

OBSTRUCTION

Charles Steweart Parnell was the greatest Irishman that ever lived only for him marrying the wrong woman, a woman he shouldn't marry from her being married before to another married man, Parnell not knowing any different from him being a Prodestan. His father was sacked from saying the Union was not right. When Charles got big he said he would put down the Union and get Home Rule. He was cold but he said he would help Mr. Joseph Bigger to make it hot for the English Parliament. So the two of them talked all day and all night until the English Parliament was falling asleep from obstruction. It made it very hard for the English Parliament to do anything. Then the people said Butt was no good, and the mantelpiece of Daniel O'Connell fell on Parnell's shoulder, and this made him the uncrownable king of Ireland. Butt soon died but he was not missed. This was pitiful.

WITHOUT NOTICE

There was a bad landlord over in Mayo named Captain Boys-cott, and the people thought of a great plan to get the three Fs. They said they would not salute him and he was ostrichised. This was like having his head buried in the sand and he did not like it. No one would hold social intercourts with him, or buy anything he had, or sell him nothing or give him the loan of a cup of sugar till tomorrow. The servant boys and servant girls left Captain Boyscott without notice. Our maid did that too and went off to England, but we are not boyscotted, this being only to have more sport in England, and shiny clothes and powder and lipstick and big words coming home to blind the neighbours.

SALUTE

The Government then said they would make the people salute Captain Boyscott and also everybody else, and they passed another Coertion Act for which the English are famous. This was not the same as Coperation. Anybody that would not salute anybody would be summonsed. Anybody that would laugh at the Government would be summonsed. The Guards in Bansha summonsed Darby Ryan's goat with bayonets fixed to her wizen. Darby Ryan made up a grand song about it, full of Oh's and it made all the people laugh, from being a satyr, making game of the pealers. Darby Ryan was a great man to make up songs and his statue is in the British Museum on account of him being the Tipperary Ministeral.

GIRLS' HELP

The people were tormented from the Coertion Act putting thousands of them in jail for mostly nothing. The Land Liege could not fight the land war from all the leaders being in jail. But all the girls made up a land liege of their own to help Michael Davitt. Michael Davitt then got married and the girls did not help him any more and Mr. Gladstone passed another Land Bill in '81 but it was only a middling one for fixing a judicial rent. Michael Davitt was a great farmers' man and the people loved him before he died, in frightful poverty, and also after, which was strange in Ireland. He tried to get the three Fs for Ireland.

FIX

Then the Government passed the Ashbin Act to give the farmers the lend of money to buy the land which was their own and then they would have the 3 Fs. They would have to pay back the money every year for 49 years and also pay money for the loan of the money, this being known as Interest. It is the chief cause of Banks, also of Security which is worse.

Mr. Gladstone was now in an awful fix for the General Election. He wanted to get the Irish votes by telling the Irish people he would give them Home Rule. He wanted to get the English votes by telling the English people he would not give the Irish people Home Rule. If he told the English people the Irish people would hear him, and if he told the Irish people, the English people would hear him. Then from trying to say he would give it and he would not, he became vague, and he said something which nobody now knows. This made him famous.

CHAMPAIGN

The Irish Party now thought of a great thing, namely the Plan of Champaign. They said they would pay the landlord a deacent rent, not rackrent, and if he would not take it he could do without nothing. Then he could not be getting drunk in England drinking champaign. This was the plan of champaign, for the three Fs.

The Government did not like this, and they said he could get drunk if he liked, so they passed another Coertion Act to let him, also to put down the Land Liege and to grind down all the people. By the virtue of this Coertion Act anybody could be summonsed for anything, and everybody in the world was laughing at the English. A little boy of ten years of age whistled a song in the street one day about Harvey Duff, not

Getting Drunk

the circulation of the blood. This frightened the life out of a magistraight who was passing and he nearly passed away, and the boy was summonsed. A man's little monkey had a little popgun for fun another day, firing it to make the people laugh, this being very good for a monkey to do; the poor little monkey was summonsed and his poor little popgun was confistcated and he never got it back. All the world laughed again at the English.

MORE LAUGHING

Another day a big man was summonsed for laughing at the Government; and he was confistcated. People did not like this, and they would not put up with it. People nowadays can laugh at the Government and they will not be summonsed because of it being a free country almost, namely a Republic almost, and all the people being left laugh when they have good reason.

Then the people were in bad humer and when the Queen's

jubbilee came on they would not please her to jubilate. The Queen also came over to Ireland one time, maybe to see what they done with her five pounds. She passed over O'Connell Bridge and all the people looked at her and they all cheered. Then she passed in to Trinity College to look at the Book of Kells and she wrote her name on the Book to let the ignorant Irish see that she could write. The Book of Kells is now in a glass case to keep vandolls from scribbling on it.

FORGE

The Times was a great and solemn paper in England, being full of big words and honour. It paid £ 2,400 for lies about Charles Stewart Parnell, saying he was fond of murder. It put the lies in the paper, being glad to get lies about Ireland, an old custom still in a good state of preservation. The lies were made up in a forge by a man named Pigott, a retch who could not spell a lot of words. *The Times* said the lying letters were not a forgery and Charles said they were.

Then a Royal Commissioner began to sit to find out the truth and make a report, and it sat for a year. It stopped sitting when Pigott confessed that he did forge the letters, then he went off to Spain to shoot himself in frightful poverty and he did, casting no gloom. Spain is a sunny land noted for bullfights and oranges. Then *The Times* got frightened and it gave Mr. Parnell £ 5,000 to say no more about the lies. The *The Times* got honourable again. It is still very honourable, not liking lies except ones about Ireland.

SPLIT

Charles Stewart Parnell now said he would get married to Mrs. O'Shea and her husband said he would not, and Charles only said what harm would it do. Then all the people got split up. Some of them said what harm, and some did not and they were called Seeseeders. Mr. Gladstone also told Mr. Parnell to give back Mrs. O'Shea, the English not liking other people's wives to be married to other people. The Bishops also said that Mr. Parnell would have to be sacked out of his job from being an immortal man, wanting another man's wife which was joined together and no man should put asunder. This caused the people to be Parnell lights and auntie Parnell lights. It was bad for Ireland and it did not increase production.

Then Parnell went off to the seaside in England to die, and he died at 45 in frightful poverty. His death would cast a gloom if it was let. He was a life long supporter of the Nationalist cause, and he is still remembered by ivy leaves. Mrs. O'Shea did not go off and die of broken heart. It is now thought that she was not very respectable. Parnell would not let no man set a march to the boundary of a nation.

PASSING THE BEER

The new century being the 20th dawned on the world at the end of the nineteenth. The history of this century cannot yet be written right owing to us not being 100 years from it so as to see it in proper perspective, namely to pick all the good bits out of all the old history books and make a new history out of

Past the Beer

them to give us national self-respect. History cannot be wrote properly until everybody who done it is dead and buried and nobody can contradict anybody.

Nevertheless the new century opened well with Queen Victoria dying with great pump and ceremony, assisted by a lot of doctors in 1901 a month after Christmas, but not, it is said, of a surfeit. After being dead a good while to let inquisitive people walk past the beer to get a look at her dead corps she got a soldier's funeral with great pump and joicing. She was well liked when she was dead, but she was a regular martingale namely a boss, letting nobody sit down while she was there and keeping down her children and telling people not to be trying to amuse her. She was however nicer than her ancestor Queen Elizabeth mainly owing to her being married Elizabeth not having got married and therefore said to be not so nice in some ways, she herself telling the people that she had the mind of a man and the might of a woman, and the Cost of Living went up.

PEACE

Queen Victoria had a great rein of peace and prosperity only for 18 wars, mostly in India, Africa and other places, the Rebecca Riots in Wales, the Chartist Riots in England, the Indian Mutiny, two risings in Ireland, and some big and small famines. This made the Queen be affectionately known in Ireland as the Famine Queen, from her giving £ 5, not of our money, to stop the big Famine and feed all the people, 2 Million of them however dying in spite of her. The 18 wars were only to kill people for their own good and bring them the blessings of English rule.

MORE PEACE

The Bowres in South Africa did not want the blessings of English rule, from being ignorant and wanting to rule themselves. The English said they would make them take the blessings and they went out to South Africa with Black and Tans and canons to civilise the people and save the natives from the Bowres. Nobody went out to save the Bowres from the English except some brave Irishmen who joined the Bowres Army. The English held two wars in South Africa, and the Bowres fought bravely. The English Black and Tans burned all the Bowres' farmhouses and then they went to relieve Lady Smith. Her husband later got a good job stitting on the Woolpack and he signed the Treaty, though having changed his name to Birkenhead.

Then the English invented concentration camps and put the Bowre women and children into them. 26,370 women and children died in them in a short time and their memoriable is to be seen to this day in Bloemfontein. This was not a nice thing to do and it made nice English people ashamed and it also gave bad example to Hitler and Stalin and Tighto.

Queen Victoria had a rein of great inventions like Sir Roland Hill inventing penny postmen and Macaroni inventing more electricity for gramophones with Sir Thomas Alvis Ediphone from America now deceased. The Cost of Living also went up.

JOLLY

Queen Victoria's biggest child Albert Edward from being born first, being 60 years of age and fat, now went up on the throne of his mother to be Edward Seventh. His Queen Alexandria, a native of Eggypt, was very unpunctuated from being nearly always late for everything and he often got vexed and said he would go without her. Albert Edward got a good chance of education at two Universities with a soldier put following him around to stop him from smoking fags, his mother not liking fags herself. Albert Edward was very jolly from being a man of the world and a great sport unknown to his mother and getting mixed up in 2 Scandals, which made him very popular and made all the people like Kings and Queens again, they being tired of Queen Victoria from her being too alufe and doing nothing to put in the Sunday papers. This can be said about Edward though he is not 100 years gone, the English people not minding what they say about their kings and making pictures about them like the private life of Henry Eighth. I would rather a cowboy picture to killing wives.

OPERATION WIND

King Edward opened the Parliament but he could not be coronated owing to a pain in his stomach. This made a lot of doctors take out his appendix and then call theirselfs fisicans to the King. This was the first appendix in the world to be took out. After that it was the custom for the big people imitating the King to have their appendix took out with a pain in the stomach even if it was only wind as babies sometimes has. The King's Appendix was preserved in the Boodling Library in Oxford for all the people to see it owing to it being a Royal appendix, also a man with two heads being preserved in the same place also in alcohol. The appendix is gone out of my history book from being torn.

BUYING

Ireland was now going ahead greatly from having no famine and they also got the Wyndham Act in 1903 to give them leaf to buy back their land from the English who robbed them of it. They could get a lend of money to do this, and the robber landlords got a present of 12 million pounds between them to coax them to sell. The Irish people also had to pay this, but only in taxes. This was the three Fs.

The Irish people were now buying too many English goods, having forgot that Dean Swift said to them to burn everything English that would not burn except English coal, some of which, however will now burn. The Irish people were also buying American bacon from America sometimes called 'the lad' at 6 ½ d. per lb., and selling their own good bacon to England at half nothing per lb. This was the cause of adverse trade balance which is not good except for T.D.'s to make big speeches about.

A FATHER

Then a new party started up in 1906 to tell the people to stop buying goods from other people to make the adverse trade balance adverser. This was called Sinn Fein, namely we ourselfs, to make people buy Irish goods and keep their money in their pockets instead of sending it over to England to make English people well off and able to keep down Ireland. This is a good policy if people would only do it, every nation now trying to do it and no one doing it, which is a good job for trade. Mr. Griffith was the father of Sinn Fein. He was a married man, and he was the greatest Irishman that ever lived. He knew a lot, especially about Hungary.

Then the University Act was passed in 1908 to stop the Royal University and start the National University above in Dublin, with constituent colleges in Cork and Galway, also a University in Belfast to give Rugby players to the Irish team. Universities was the main cause of medical students, now however not so bad from being scarcer owing to hard examinations and being hunted home after failing often.

LAYING

Mr. Askwit was now Prime Minister and he said he would ask Home Rule for Ireland. So he laid a Bill in 1912 before the House. He also laid a foundation stone another time. The Bill was to give Ireland their own Parliament in Dublin to rule Ireland, and if they tried to make a law the Lord Leftenant or the English Parliament would have power to stop them. This was known as Home Rule. The Unanists being a small minority nevertheless said they would not have this Bill and they said they would sign a paper called a Covnant against it. Then the Lords threw the Bill out and the Commonses threw it in again.

DISTURBANCE

The Great War broke out gradually in 1914 by a man shooting a man dead on his holydays in Sarajeevo, and it was a great disturbance in many places. The man that shot the man was a student, some students having bad manners. The man that the man shot belonged to big people from him being air-presumption to the Austrian throne. The people of Austra did not like this and they wrote a note to the people of Sarajeevo to tell them to pay for his funeral and other things. The Sarajeevoes said they would not pay and Germany then said they would back up Austria to make the Sarajeevoes pay. Then the Sarajeevoes said they would pay but Austria becoming vexed said they would not take no money, but they would fight a war. Nobody knows who caused the war, it not being 100 years gone.

TEARS

Then Germany said they would fight a war too and send a nultimatum to Russia. The people of Russia at once hit back at Germany with a steam roller. This caused more war and it also made the Russian steam roller famous. Russian roads are very good in places though long and frozen.

Then the English bravely said they would not let nobody touch little Belgium. Germany said she would touch little Belgium if she liked, and she did. Then all England cried for sorrow for little Belgium and began to gather an army. Then Germany said the English was nothing but a pack of hippocrits pretending to be fond of little Belgium on a scrap of paper and grinding down little Ireland which England has no right to do. Governments are the cause of wars but they do not fight in them. The war made the cost of living go up.

A CHANCE

Many Irishmen pitied little Belgium and went off singing from their wives, to fight for small nations. This was the cause of separation women in Ireland, getting 29 shillings a week while their husband was fighting somebody else, and a chance of fifty pounds if he got shot, as many did in the Dardanelles and other places.

Most Irish people, however, would not go out to fight England's battles from knowing that England was always our enemy and Germany was not. Then England said they would coax Irishmen out by letting Home Rule stay on the Statue Book and after the war was over they would atomatically pass it.

SPLIT

A split now grew up in the Volunteers, and this was known as the Split from them being split up among themselves. Mr. Redmond was the Irish leader and he said Ireland would back up England in the war, to get Home Rule maybe. We cannot yet say things about Mr. Redmond from him not being in proper perspective not being 100 years ago. Irish people often got split up like other people, and like the English people,

Split in the Volunteers

hunting Mr. Lied George after one war and Mr. Churchill after another war.

Then Mr. Griffith said Ireland would not back up England because Ireland was not at war with nobody, and had no reason to fight for England with her bad Home Rule on a Statue Book, and she out fighting for freedom of small nations and no freedom for Ireland, which was only hippocracy.

PROPER PERSPECTIVE

Then Sinn Fein being ourselfs said the right place to fight for the freedom of small nations was at home in Ireland for the freedom of our own small nation enslaved by England. They were led by Patrick Pearse who was the greatest Irishman that ever lived, giving everything he had and also his life for Ireland. He died for Ireland before anyone had time to turn against him and so he is in proper perspective, not having to wait 100 years. Pearse was the main cause of the movement. Pearse was backed up by James Connolly who was the greatest Irishman that ever lived. He gave a party for workmen in Dublin now known as the Labour Party and when it was over they said they would fight for Ireland. This was good for the movement.

FOR FREEDOM

All the Volunteers marched in 1916 and took Dublin. They hunted all the clerks out of the General's Post Office and fortificated the building with books and other buildings as well. Then they gave out the Proclamation saying that Ireland belonged to the Irish people and the Irish people would rule it. This was the best part of the movement. England did not like this from being only in the habit of fighting for the freedom of little Belgium instead of little Ireland. So they sent over thousands of soldiers and big guns and battleships which were badly wanted to fight for the freedom of little Belgium, and they told them to blow up little Dublin and crush little Ireland. They said little Ireland stabbed them in the back, their back not yet being up again the wall as it was later on.

CHIVALRY

The Irish Volunteers fought bravely for a week, being a mere handful against the mighty and proud British Empire. Then they had to surrender. The British said the Irish Volunteers had too small an army to be called an army and so they would not keep the rules of war, only shoot their prisoners like dogs up against the wall. They shot the Irish leaders who were prisoners. James Connolly was badly wounded in the leg and he could not stand up to be shot like a dog. A kind British officer brought out a chair for him to sit on while being shot. This is known as British chivalry. Sixteen brave Irish soldiers were shot for fighting for the freedom of Ireland, and then the British soldiers went off again to fight for the freedom of small nations, the British still being full of chivalry. But the British could not stop the movement.

SAYING NOTHING

A lot of Irishmen were now took over and put into English jails to stop them from thinking that Ireland should get freedom. This made Irishmen stop going out to fight England's war. This was bad for England because Englishmen would not go out and fight either even when promised farms, having to be made to do so by conscription. Mr. Lied George was the English Minister and he said he would make the Irish go. We must not say anything about the sort of twister Mr. Lied George was, from him not yet being a 100 years over, and not in proper perspective. The Irish would not have Mr. Lied George's Conscription and the Bishops of Ireland said they need not have it because it was a nopressive and unjust law. This was a great help for the movement.

SONG

Lied George could do nothing then only try to conscript Englishmen to fight for their own country. He said he would try another trick in Ireland, Mr. Lied George being full of crooked tricks of which we must not mention from him not being 100 years dead and buried. He said he would postbone Conscription in Ireland if only 50,000 Irishmen would only go out and kill Germans to save England and let Englishmen stay at home safe. The Irish people only laughed at Mr. Lied George and the Irish Unanists got vexed but not many of them went out to fight. The Irish people told Mr. Lied George to sing a long way to Tipperary a new way, to get soldiers, namely

> 'Come forward the fifty thousand, get into kharkee
> We will give you all a farm, and a guarantee
> The dimensions of the farm will be six feet by three
> We don't know if you'll get the D.S.O., but you're sure of the R.I.P.'

Songs like this was to be heard everywhere during the movement.

LEADER

The English were now getting beat by the Germans from the English leader doing nothing only having his back up against a wall, his name also being Haig. The English was great for singing songs in the war like Keep the whole fire burning, and there's a long long trail a winding, and Paddy McGinty's goat, but they were not so good for fighting. So at last they coaxed America to come, and the Americans came in 1917 when the war was three years going on and everybody tired, this being a clever plan of America in wars, known as strategy. They could not beat the Germans however, from General Haig not being able to come away from the wall, the Americans and the British having no good leader. Then they got a good leader from France named General Foch.

PEACE

The English and Americans did not like General Foch for a leader, but they had to take him and he finished off the war in seven months, and Germany having no more guns and bullets could not keep on fighting nearly the whole world. The English then said they won the war themselves and the Americans said they did not, but they both said they would shut up about it and they held a meeting near Paris to make Germany pay for everything, namely Riparations. President Wilson was the head man of America and he had 14 pints before the meeting but nobody took any notice of him, so they made the Treaty of

113

Versay which pleased nobody, later causing more wars. Germany had to pay everything she had, but England would not pay America the money she owed. There was also a great League of Nations started to give freedom to every nation except Ireland, namely selfdetermination.

FAIR PLAY

Ireland now said they should get freedom as well as little Belgium and all the other countries, but England said they should not. America, albeit a country loving freedom, backed up England, this being known as might is right, and different from fair-play. Then Ireland said she would fight to drive the English out of her country, and the Irish fought bravely with hardly no arms, only a few rifles and shot guns, and the English could not beat them, from it being gorilla warfare. The English used to ambush the Irish with armoured cars and loose guns and Crossley tenders and lorries and everything. The Irish had nothing to ambush the English only walls and ditches. The English said it was not fair to go behind a ditch, but they said it was fair to go behind an armoured car, and have loose guns and machine guns and thousands of soldiers against a few untrained men with only rifles and not enough amonition. This did not help the movement.

MORE FAIR PLAY

England executed all the Irish prisoners of war which she captured in the war. The Irish army did not execute prisoners. There is no rules of war or of anything for a big nation fighting a small nation only the law of the jungle namely might is right, like the wolf and the lamb. Then England sent over Black and Tans, namely criminals let out of English jails, these being the drags of the population, to shoot all they liked. They used to get mad drunk to give them courage to go out, and then they went around the country murdering men and women and also priests and children and burning houses towns and villages like they did in South Africa, only worse. They were told to do this by their leaders like Mr. Smyth telling them in Listowel to shoot all round them and if they made mistakes and shot people who did not need shooting it would be no harm. The I.R.A. took this advice once, and shot Mr. Smyth dead. He did not like this, not knowing that he needed shooting.

TREATY

The decent English people now got ashamed of what was done by England in Ireland, there being a good many decent people in England who have nothing to do with politics. They told Lied George to stop disgracing England because America and everyone else was talking about them. Lied George then stopped because he did not want to disgrace England and because he could not win the war in Ireland, and because he was afraid that America might get vexed and ask England to pay her debts, which she did not, America not caring much more about small nations than England. Mr. Churchill wanted to murder all the Irish, to stop the movement.

Then Mr. Lied George said to the Irish to come over and make a Treaty with him, and some brave Irishmen did. Then they brought home the Treaty and a lot of Irishmen at home said it was no good and they would not take it. Mr. Griffith and Mr. Collins was the two greatest Irishmen that ever lived and they said they would take the Treaty because it was a good one, they having signed it themselves. Nobody can yet say whether Mr. Griffith and Mr. Collins was right or wrong from their not being dead 100 years, and so nobody mentions it. England kept six of our counties in the North of Ireland and would not give them back, but we will get them yet. This is now known as Partition, which lets everybody know the sort England is.

NEUTRAL

Mr. De Valera was the greatest Irishman that ever lived and he said he would not take the Treaty, which was no good. Nobody can yet say whether Mr. De Valera was wrong or right until he will be 100 years gone and people can find out the truth which will make no difference then, it not making much difference even now, so nobody mentions it. A lot of books have been wrote to tell people who was right and who was wrong. One half of the country does not believe one half of the books and the other half of the country does not believe the other half. The other half of the country does not believe neither half. All history books should be newteral for 100 years, from not knowing what happened. Then people who was not there at all can guess what happened in proper perspective and write proper history books which are not newteral.

PAPERS PLEASED

Then there was a great split in Ireland. The Dail was split up in to two big halfs, with one half a little bit bigger than the other. This split the country into two big halfs too. One half said they would rule the country and the other half said they would not let them. All the English soldiers went off home out of Ireland and all the Unanists was broken-hearted, so see them going.

Then fighting started in Ireland and the English papers was very pleased, saying the Irish was always fighting among themselves and could not rule theirselves. The Irish said it was the English was always fighting among theirselfs except when they were fighting other people to take their lands, the English having a Civil War in the time of King John, also a Civil Wars of the Rosies for 40 years, also a big long Civil War in the time of King Charles I, being murdered fowly by his own subjects. English papers still like to run down Ireland.

LIGHT

The war in Ireland went on for a while, Mr. Griffith dying and Mr. Collins getting shot, which was a pity. Then Mr. Cosgrave said he would rule Ireland with two houses, namely Dail Erin and Seanad Erin. Dail Erin is for to get into by votes and Seanad Erin is for people who would not be let into Dail Erin. Mr. Cosgrave ruled Ireland very well until 1932, making many good laws and putting on more taxes and the country went ahead greatly, the cost of living going up. No one can yet say anything about Mr. Cosgrave from him not being 100 years gone.

This was a time of great scientific advance from teachers salaries and Old Age pensions being cut and the E.S.B. being invented to give all the people light. Some of the people have not light yet, and maybe never will see the light, some people says. The light is dear enough from coming through a metre.

SWEARING

All this time Mr. De Valera and his men stayed outside the Dail because they would not swear. Then Mr. Cosgrave said they should come in or go away, and he said he would let nobody go for the Dail if he could not swear. So Mr. De Valera and his men then swore, but they did it their own way with mental preservation namely an empty formalin. They said if the people would vote for them they would have no more oats to

England and they would not pay the land Amnesties. This was money to pay England for giving back the land she robbed from Ireland. The people said they would vote for Mr. De Valera and they did and then Mr. De Valera and his men got to be the Government, in 1932, and they ruled very well, putting on more taxes.

HEALTHY

Mr. De Valera and his men now done away with swearing and they got a new Constitution. This made all the people very healthy. Then Mr. De Valera would not pay the land Amnesties to England. The English did not like Mr. De Valera for not giving them money for the land that they robbed and for wanting to keep the money in ·Ireland. England having also robbed Ireland of three hundred million pounds too much in taxes. England then put a big tax on Irish cattle going over to England of six pounds on every one. This went on a long time but the Irish farmers would not give in to England and so they ate all the cattle themself. This was a great time for all the people from eating cheap cattle and sheep. Then the English had to make a settlement, to get food from Ireland, and this stopped snuggling across the border.

BROADCASTED

Kinge George Fifth now got sick after Christmas in 1936 and he died. In this he was greatly assisted by the B.B.C. at his bedside to tell all the people he was getting worse and worse until his life egged away. This was a great time for the B.B.C. because of him not being burried for a good while and all the people foiling past the beer. King George was the first King to die by means of the B.B.C., being broadcasted to his grave owing to modern science. A lot of people went to his funeral though he was not burried for a good while. The B.B.C. made everyone lonesome after him. He was exceeded by his oldest son on the throne, then known as Edward the Eighth.

LOVE

Edward the Eighth was called Davy at home. He was very jolly from falling off horses and going to dances and foreign countries and having great sport in America, from the papers there saying prince comes home with the milkman, and his father did not like this while he was alive. Kings have nothing to do now only fill up forms and open hospitals and things, not like long ago when they could cut off their wife's heads and burn all the people at the steak. King Edward thus had not so much sport when he got to be King, from having to be very respectable, but he ruled very well, being single, and then he said he would marry a woman with two husbands from America, Americans also being very jolly. The Prime Minister was Mr. Baldwing and he said the King could not marry a married woman from America, this not being good for the British constitution. The King said he could if he liked, not caring for Mr. Baldwing or his constitution. Then Mr. Baldwing said the King would have to give up his job and this was known as Abdictation. It was also a Crisis. The King said he would give up his job from not being able to cut off Mr. Baldwing's head or burn him at the steak which many people in England said would be good enough for him. Then the King said to the B.B.C. that he would go off to the 1 he loved in a destroyer in the dark. This he did and all the people was talking about the Abductation but he got married in spite of them to the 1 he loved when she got away from another husband, and they lived happily ever afterwards everywhere except in England. Other sacked Kings live everywhere too except at home.

PANSIES

The Great War was begun in 1939 and it was a great disturbance in many places. Some people say it was started by somebody and other people say it was started by somebody else. Nobody can say rightly for 100 years, when everybody who knows about it will be dead.

Mr. Hitler was the head man in German and he was the greatest German that ever lived. He had a strong army made up of guns and butter and all marching with legs like geese. He had many Pansy divisions and he called them very early one morning before anybody was awake. They all got up and they got out their tanks, and drove off into Poland and killed all the people.

NAMES

Then England cried with sorrow for poor Poland and said she would be behind her in the fight, and she stayed behind her and done nothing. Then the war spread out, but the French was very safe behind the Madgino Line down in holes under the ground. Hitler did not fight fair and come over to the Madgino Line and get killed. He went around the end of it and walked into France, putting many big bulges in the French army. This was the end of the Madgino Line. Then Hitler chased home the English army who was out in France. They came home without their luggage from Dunkirk being in a great hurry, and Hitler took France. Mr. Churchill frightened all the Germans with great speeches and calling names, calling Moss O'Leeny a tattered jackass from Italy because Moss O'Leeny was helping Hitler.

MIXED

Then the war got bigger, Russia attacking Finland because Finland was small, also taking half of Poland before Germany could grab it all. England helped Finland against Russia by sending them guns. Nobody helped the poor Polands. Later England helped Russia to fight Germany. Big nations do not care about right or wrong only to do what suits them. England done her best to get America into the war, America being a big powerful land. America said she would stay safe at home, but she would give England guns and things and she did, from wanting to see Germany beat, but letting someone else beat it. She also gave England ships, all the English ships being sunk by German submarines.

Then Hitler's patience got exhausted and he went into Russia one morning very early. This was against the packed he had with Russia. England then forgot about Finland and Poland and helped Russia. The war was now very mixed, from Mr. Hitler's patience getting exhausted often and Mr. Churchill calling more names. Calling names is forbidden by the Fifth Commandment.

YELLOW?

Then the Japaneses blew up all the Americans one morning at Peril Harbour very early before the Americans was up. This was not fair, sinking all their ships with boms so early in the morning before the Americans was awoke, and never telling them first that they were going to do it. America had to go in to the war then after 2 ¼ years to save herself, instead of looking on and giving guns to others to fight. This made America feel very brave, and she said everybody else should be in the war too such as Ireland! All the papers in America now got brave too and said Ireland was yellow not to go and fight. Ireland only laughed at this from knowing that America did not fight until she could not help it. Ireland said she would mind her own business and not go fighting nobody who did nothing to her, she having no enemy but England, keeping our 6 counties. Mr. Churchill wanted to get Irish ports for his ships to get us all bommed, and he was mad when Mr. De Valera would not give them, and he made more speeches. He also said never did so many in England owe so much money to a few. This was because the Cost of Living went up.

FROLIC

Then England got some great generals, also America. A great general always wins battles by being very clever, namely by having 5 times as many soldiers and guns and everything as the enemy. So Germany not having enough soldiers ,and guns and things had to give up. Mr. Churchill was full up of himself, saying England stood alone, and America only laughed. Then Mr. Churchill made a ugly speech about Ireland and Mr. De Valera frolicking with a German minister. This was because we would not fight Mr. Churchill's war for him. Mr. De Valera gave Mr. Churchill his answer one night on the wireless telling him Ireland stood alone for seven hundred years. This was the greatest speech that ever lived and everyone listened to it, and also Mr. Churchill. He had no answer and so he said no more about Ireland.

COLD WAR

Then England and America made prisoners of all the German leaders and they killed them all. They did not, however, eat them, as some cannibles do. They also killed Lord Ha Ha for talking against them on the wireless and calling names, like Mr. Churchill.

Then the English and the Americans and the Russians made big treaties among themselves to which they could not agree, no big nation trusting no other big nation, from knowing that might is right.

Then the world was very quiet and peaceful except for wars in Korea and Indo-China and other places, and also the cold war with Russia, the climate of that country being all snow, especially in Siberia, a good place for banishing people. Then all the big nations started to get ready for the next big war. It will be the biggest war yet and it will not be cold. They have fine new boms and guns and guided missles to kill millions together. The next war will also be a war to end all wars, and it is said that it will also end all the people.

JOBBERY

Ireland was now going ahead greatly from having its own Republic above in Dublin with thirty-six hundred thousand Civil Servants to govern us right. This is to give jobs to all the people's children and it is sometimes called jobbery. The Government of Ireland is to rule 26/32ths of Ireland well and to give money to all the people. It is also to take heavy taxes from the Civil Servants, namely Income Tax. This is not taking back a lot of their salaries, it is only Income Tax. Farmers do not pay Income Tax and Civil Servants do not make them, it being too hard, from farmers being the backbone of the country, and very hard. My father do not like Income Tax. He would like to be a farmer.

QUEEN

George VI had got to be King from being brother to Edward the Eight but he was fairly delikit though being a nice man from having a wife of his own and some children and good for staying at home, viz., home life. He had a big operation which was long over and then one night he died of something else not so serious, unknown to the B.B.C., and he was woke up dead in the morning. His daughter was gone away on her holidays but she came home to the funeral after getting a telegram and she was made into a Queen from being the first of George the Sixth. She is a very nice young girl with a husband of her own and some children, but he must walk behind her. They are always getting their fotos took but they are not stuck up at all, like other people.

SIX THIRTYTWOS

Queen Elizabeth was coronated with great pump and a procession by the B.B.C. and the Archbishop of Canterbury. She had a very nice dress on her. Millions of people slept out on the streets in the rain in London where it is always raining, to see the procession. This is known as British endurance, also mass histeria. It was however good for the B.B.C. from Queen Elizabeth being the first Queen to be televisioned. Mr. Churchill made the Queen say she is the Queen of Our Six Counties, this being the first time anyone was coronated Queen of 6/32ths of a country. The Irish told Mr. Churchill to think of the speech he made in 1912 saying that Ulster 'cannot stand in the way of the whole of the rest of Ireland. Half a province cannot impose a permanent veto on the nation. Half a province cannot obstruct for ever the reconciliation between British and Irish democracies and deny all satisfaction to the United wishes of the British Empire.' We have Mr. Churchill's speech for a recitation in school but Mr. Churchill does not care. Queen Elizabeth is now a very good Queen of England and loved by all her people and this will keep Communism from going ahead in England. This was a time of great scientific advance from two men going up through the snow to the top of Mount Everest and leaving Chocolate and other things there, which was a pity.

PROSPEROUS

Ireland was now very prosperous from being able to give doals and pensions to all the people. Doals is sometimes called grants and subcities. Some people can get money for boots and for being sick or old. Some can get money for being idle and some for having children. This is known as Sociable Welfare. One child is no good but three is worth £. 1 8. 6. every month in the Post Office. Children is good for a country, but some people do not like them. Farmers can get money for everything, namely for cowsheds, gates, wheat, beet, butter and digging dykes and everything. This is known as grants and subcities to coax farmers to set the crops and milk the cows. Farmers are now very rich, but grumbling, from having to buy motor cars for their children to go mad around the country, spending the big money.

FREEDOM

This is because Ireland has a lot of T.D's and they have great pull. T.D's have not to pass a examination and they must not pass the doctor nor know Oral Irish nor anything, only get enough No. 1s and also No. 2s. T.D's. are very nice men however, and also a few women. They do not praise themselves, only tell the people about the good they done so that the people would know about it. They shake hands with everybody always and they do not call one another names like liars and rats and things, like other people do. If they did, it would be put into the papers the first thing viz. 'Scene in the Dail,' and it would be the first thing everyone would read. If the T.D's done this they would have to be sorry, or else they would be threw out of the Dail, for a day or two. This is known as the Dignity of the House. T.D.'s. can however, say anything they like about anybody and they cannot be summonsed. This is a sign of demockrasy and it is known as Freedom from Fear. There are also other freedoms, invented by Mr. Roosevelt.

OPPOSITION

Some T.D.'s. is the Government and some is the Opposition. The Government is to pass things to rule the country and the Opposition is to stop them. They get paid for this. The Government is bigger than the Opposition. The Opposition do not like this, and they are always saying that everything in the country is rotten and the Government saying it is grand. Then the Opposition gets bigger than the Government and the Government is the Opposition and the Opposition is the Government and the Government that was the Opposition says everything is grand that was rotten and the Opposition that was the Government says everything is rotten that was grand which is the opposite, politicians not minding what they say. The people can say nothing, only pay the taxes.

REVIVAL

The Irish language was now loved by everybody and spoke by nobody except A Cairde Gael to begin a speech. This was known as the Irish Revival. Irish is, however, spoke in National Schools and also at examinations in Oral Irish, such as Cad as tu. This is so that boys and girls from the Gaeltacht can get good marks and scholarships from knowing Irish in spite of theirselfs. Then they can come out of the Gaeltacht where Irish is dying, and they need not speak it no more. Other boys and girls work hard to learn Irish but they can not get such good marks. This is from not having the bloss, viz. talking very quick and hard to understand. Ireland will soon be Irish-speaking again when the Ministers and the T.D's and all the people speak Irish. This is because Eduacation is very good in Ireland from having Universities to make doctors for England and also very high eduacation viz. the School of Comic Physicks to tell all the people what kind of weather we had last month.

HOME LIFE

Ireland was now full of societies and clubs and associations and partys and organisations and unions and federations and macras and cumanns. These were for the good of everybody and all the people were in them. This made Ireland very jolly and it put an end to home life. Everyone now also has a motor car for going to dances and races and football matches. Ireland is famous for racehorses, being sold for nearly nothing and then bought back again for nearly millions, of our money. This brings a lot of foreign men to Ireland to look for cheap race horses.

BEGORRAH!

Ireland now had a great tourist trade, from the country being the most lovely in the world, and some lovely people in it too. A lot of English people come over for their holidays to Ireland. They talk very loud and have a good time, from getting enough to eat, especially meat. Some English people are pleased to see cities and towns and roads and railways and airports in Ireland. Some of them go looking for fairies and knee breeches and spalpeens and barefooted colleens and the pig in the parlour. Some of them go talking to the peasants to hear them saying Bedad and Begorrah and bejabers. They do not like it when they do not say it. This is from reading their own newspapers and going to plays at the Abbey. The Irish people tell the English people many funny stories which they believe. Then they buy lots of things in Ireland and go home very pleased and tell other English people that barefut savages is very scarce in Ireland. This is not good for the tourist trade from keeping other English people at home because of there not being enough savages in Ireland for them to look at. American people also come to Ireland. They also talk very loud and ask the price of everything and buy nothing. This is from everyone wanting to rob Americans. They do not stay long in Ireland, from everything in it being too small for them. Americans also being always in a hurry.

GOOD HEALTH

Ireland is now a very healthy country from having many good health Bills in the Dail. Doctors do not like good Health Bills, from not liking to have nobody sick and saying everybody should be let sick if they like. People who are sick can now go to hospital to die in great comfort assisted by doctors and nurses. This is why infantile morality is now very low in Ireland. It is different from the time when everybody in Ireland was dying of T.B. and also diptera.

CHANGE

Ireland was now going ahead greatly from Muncher na Tire being spread all over the country, including Belfast, and all the Orange Men being in it. This made the Orange Men like people they never liked before and this was the end of Partition. Ireland now had one big Government in Dublin with Orange Men in it and the north people of Ireland done all the business of the South. Then the north people all got into the Dail from being good at business. They ruled Ireland very well and put on more taxes. All the people of Cork went home from Dublin and won more All-Irelands. Then the Dublin Corporation put on more taxes to make more roads out of Dublin.

MORE TAXES

Then the people from the North all got converted to the true faith by great Irish missioners from the South. This was because of St. Patrick being from the North, namely Antrim. Then all the great Irish missioners from the North and the South went off to foreign countries like England and Russia and China and Japan, and converted them all except America, and Ireland then ruled them all very well, putting on more taxes. No one could convert America, from the Americans being in too big a hurry to listen. Then no more people would go over to America and all the people of America died out and the grass grew over the skyscrapers of New York, grass growing very big in America. Then more Irish people went over to America to cut the grass, Irish people having then got to be good farmers and fond of land. Then Ireland had five provinces, namely Munster, Leinster, Ulster, Connacht and America, and they ruled them very well, putting on more taxes. This made the Dail bigger, but it assisted trade. There was no more wars and no more History, and the World got on very well until the Last Day, and then the Cost of Living went down, and the balance of payments went up, and nobody put on no more taxes. This was the end of all the people, in frightful poverty.

ARCHBISHOP MAGRATH,
The Scoundrel of Cashel
Robert Wyse Jackson

Milar Magrath was appointed Bishop of Down and Connor in 1565 by the Pope. Later he was invested by Queen Elizabeth I as Protestant Archbishop of Cashel and for a number of years successfully held both opposing positions and drew revenues from each Diocese.

In Irish eyes he has always been referred to as that 'wicked Archbishop, a notorious manipulator and trimmer, the man you love to hate.' And yet as Dr Jackson probes the character of Milar one cannot help feeling something like affection for him.

He lived for 100 years, and by so doing came near to spanning the gulf between the bloodthirsty world of medieval Ireland and the polished Anglo-Irish elite of Berkeley and Swift.

AND SO BEGAN
Seamus Wilmot

In this age of stereotypes, which seeks to classify everything, it is exciting to come on a book which defies all labels. Cast in the classic satiric mould, it is a parable of a man, a country, and a language.

LETTERS OF A SUCCESSFUL T.D.
John B. Keane

This bestseller takes a humourous peep at the correspondence of an Irish parliamentary deputy. Keane's eyes have fastened on the human weakness of a man who secured power through the ballot box, and uses it to ensure the comfort of his family and friends.

LETTERS OF AN IRISH PARISH PRIEST
John B. Keane

There is a riot of laughter in every page and its theme is the correspondence between a country parish priest and his nephew who is studying to be a priest. Father O'Mora has been referred to by one of his parishioners as one who 'is suffering from an overdose of racial memory aggravated by religious bigotry.' John B. Keane's humour is neatly pointed, racy of the soil and never forced. This book gives a picture of a way of life which though in great part is vanishing is still familiar to many of our countrymen who still believe 'that priests could turn them into goats.' It brings out all the humour and pathos of Irish life. It is hilariously funny and will entertain and amuse everyone.

LETTERS OF A MATCHMAKER
John B. Keane

These are the letters of a country matchmaker faithfully recorded by John B. Keane, whose knowledge of matchmaking is second to none.

In these letters is revealed the unquenchable, insatiable longing that smoulders unseen under the mute, impassive faces of our batchelor brethren.

Comparisons may be odious but readers will find it fascinating to contrast the Irish matchmaking system with that of the 'Cumangettum Love Parlour' in Philadelphia. They will meet many unique characters from the Judas Jennies of New York to Finnuala Crust of Coomasahara who buried two giant-sized, sexless husbands but eventually found happiness with a pint-sized jockey from North Cork.

LETTERS OF A LOVE-HUNGRY FARMER
John B. Keane

John B. Keane has introduced a new word into the English language — 'chastitute'. This is the story of a chastitute, i.e. a man who has never lain down with a woman for reasons which are fully disclosed within this book. It is the tale of a lonely man who will not humble himself to achieve his heart's desire, whose need for female companionship whines and whimpers throughout. Here are the hilarious sex escapades of John Bosco McLane culminating finally in one dreadful deed.

LETTERS OF AN IRISH PUBLICAN
John B. Keane

In this book we get a complete picture of life in Knock-anee as seen through the eyes of a publican, Martin MacMeer. He relates his story to his friend Dan Stack who is a journalist. He records in a frank and factual way events like the cattle fair where the people 'came in from the hinterland with caps and ash-plants and long coats', and the cattle stood 'outside the doors of the houses in the public streets.'

Through his remarkable perception we 'get a tooth' for all the different characters whom he portrays with sympathy, understanding and wit. We are overwhelmed by the charms of the place where at times 'trivial incidents assume new proportions.' These incidents are exciting, gripping, hilarious, touching and uncomfortable.

Send us your name and address if you would like to receive our complete catalogue of books of Irish Interest.

THE MERCIER PRESS
4 Bridge Street, Cork, Ireland